THE BIBLE TIMELINE FOR MIDDLE SCHOOL
ENCOUNTER

STUDENT WORKBOOK

Mark Hart

with Colin and Aimee MacIver

West Chester, Pennsylvania

Nihil obstat: Rev. Robert A. Pesarchick, STD
                    Censor librorum
                    December 18, 2023

Imprimatur: + Most Rev. Nelson J. Perez, DD
                    Archbishop of Philadelphia
                    December 21, 2023

© 2024 Ascension Publishing Group, LLC. All rights reserved.

With the exception of short excerpts used in articles and critical reviews, no part of this work may be reproduced, transmitted, or stored in any form whatsoever, printed or electronic, without the prior written permission of the publisher.

Excerpts from the English translation of the *Catechism of the Catholic Church* for use in the United States of America © 1994 United States Catholic Conference, Inc.–Libreria Editrice Vaticana. Used by permission. English translation of the *Catechism of the Catholic Church: Modifications from the Editio Typica* © 1997 United States Conference of Catholic Bishops–Libreria Editrice Vaticana.

Unless otherwise noted, Scripture passages are from the Revised Standard Version of the Bible–Second Catholic Edition (Ignatius Edition) © 2006 National Council of the Churches of Christ in the United States of America. Used by permission. All rights reserved.

The Great Adventure® and *The Bible Timeline*® are registered trademarks of Ascension Publishing Group, LLC.

Ascension
PO Box 1990
West Chester, PA 19380
1-800-376-0520
ascensionpress.com

Cover design: Chris Lewis, BARITUS Catholic; Stella Ziegler; and Sarah Stueve

Printed in the United States of America

ISBN: 978-1-954882-50-8

Contents

A Letter from Mark Hart...1

Lesson One
INTRODUCTION TO THE BIBLE..2

Lesson Two
EARLY WORLD...16

Lesson Three
PATRIARCHS – EGYPT...32

Lesson Four
EXODUS – DESERT WANDERINGS – CONQUEST & JUDGES...............................48

Lesson Five
ROYAL KINGDOM – DIVIDED KINGDOM..................................64

Lesson Six
EXILE – RETURN – MACCABEAN REVOLT................................80

Lesson Seven
MESSIANIC FULFILLMENT: JESUS AND THE GOSPELS...................94

Lesson Eight
THE CHURCH (AND YOUR ROLE IN IT)...................................110

Glossary..124

Further Resources...128

About the Authors and Presenters...148

Program Credits..150

A Letter from Mark Hart

There are a lot of ways you can get to know people, but nothing works like sitting with someone one-on-one and talking together. That person can't really know you, either, until you share from your heart.

There is one important exception. There is someone who already knows all about you, someone who loves you more than life itself. I'm not talking about Santa Claus or about your parents. I'm talking about God, the author of your life.

That's right: God is the Author of Life, and you are a character in his story. If you really want to know yourself, the best way to do that is to get to know the Father who created you.

The Bible is a great way to get to know God and the kind of Father he is. You'll also get to know a lot of his children. Everyone you encounter in the Bible is worth learning from in some way. You'll soon realize that living as a Christian is not so much about "finding yourself"; it's more about finding and unleashing Christ's power within you. And the more you recognize God's presence in your life, the better you'll be able to share his love with others.

The secret to a joyful life and a hope-filled future isn't about figuring out tomorrow. It's about listening to God *today*.

God, the Author of Life, has something to say to you through the brothers and sisters who went before you. So take a deep breath and turn the page—it's story time!

God bless you,

Mark Hart

Lesson One
Introduction to the Bible

The Big Picture

The Bible isn't just a book *about God*. The Bible is God's own Word—the Word *of God*. There is a huge difference between a book that describes God and a book that is a direct message from him to us.

Even better, that message from God is about how deeply he loves us—then, now, always. Sacred Scripture isn't just a history lesson; it wasn't meant only for people who lived long ago. When you learn the story of God's people, you are learning your own story as well.

OPENING PRAYER

"God our Father, you gave us your Word so that we could know and encounter you. You also gave us your Word so that we could know our own story—who we are and how to grow close to you. Speak to us through your Word. Make this encounter real and lasting in our lives. In Jesus' name, we pray. Amen."

REMEMBER THIS!

"Let no one despise your youth, but set the believers an example in speech and conduct, in love, in faith, in purity."

—1 Timothy 4:12

You are young, just like St. Timothy was when St. Paul wrote to him. Paul was reminding Timothy that holiness does not depend on age.

When Paul wrote these words almost two thousand years ago, God knew that you would read them today. God wanted to give you a personal message with these words: *He's calling* you, *and you are capable of teaching and inspiring everyone around you.*

In the same way that I (Mark) learned this verse long ago, you can memorize it and, more importantly, live by it as an example for others. How?

- In the way you talk, text, and post
- In the way you act 24/7
- In the way you put others ahead of yourself
- In the way you honor your body and everyone around you
- In the way you believe in God and trust him

WARM UP

Fun Fill-in-the-Blanks

Sacred Scripture is the story of God's people. In the Bible, we encounter many unique men and women, each with his or her own story. Their adventures and failures, guided patiently by God's plan, form the ultimate story that is salvation history.

You are also one of God's people, living your own story. Let's learn more about each other so that together we can learn more about God.

Fill in the blanks:

1. I was born in _____.
2. My name is _____.
3. My parents' names are _____.
4. My siblings' or friends' names are _____.
5. My favorite outfit is _____.
6. My favorite food is _____.
7. A positive way to describe myself is _____.
8. My favorite animal is _____.
9. A place I want to visit is _____.
10. A group of people I want to help or serve is _____.
11. My favorite toy, stuffed animal, or activity when I was little was _____.

Now plug your responses into the following story. Each member of the group can share.

In that time, in the land of (1)_____, there was born a child named (2)_____. He/She was the son/daughter of (3)_____ and the sibling/friend of (4)_____. As he/she grew in strength and wisdom, he/she wore (5)_____ and fed upon (6)_____. Among all the youth in the land, there were few so (7)_____ as (2)_____. One day, while he/she was tending his/her flock of (8)_____, an angel of the Lord appeared. The angel said, "Fear not! God is with you. Go to the land of (9)_____ and bring good news to the (10)_____." So (2)_____ went forth, with (11)_____ in hand, to bring good news from the Lord. (And this is only the beginning!)

TIME PERIOD OVERVIEW

The Bible Timeline

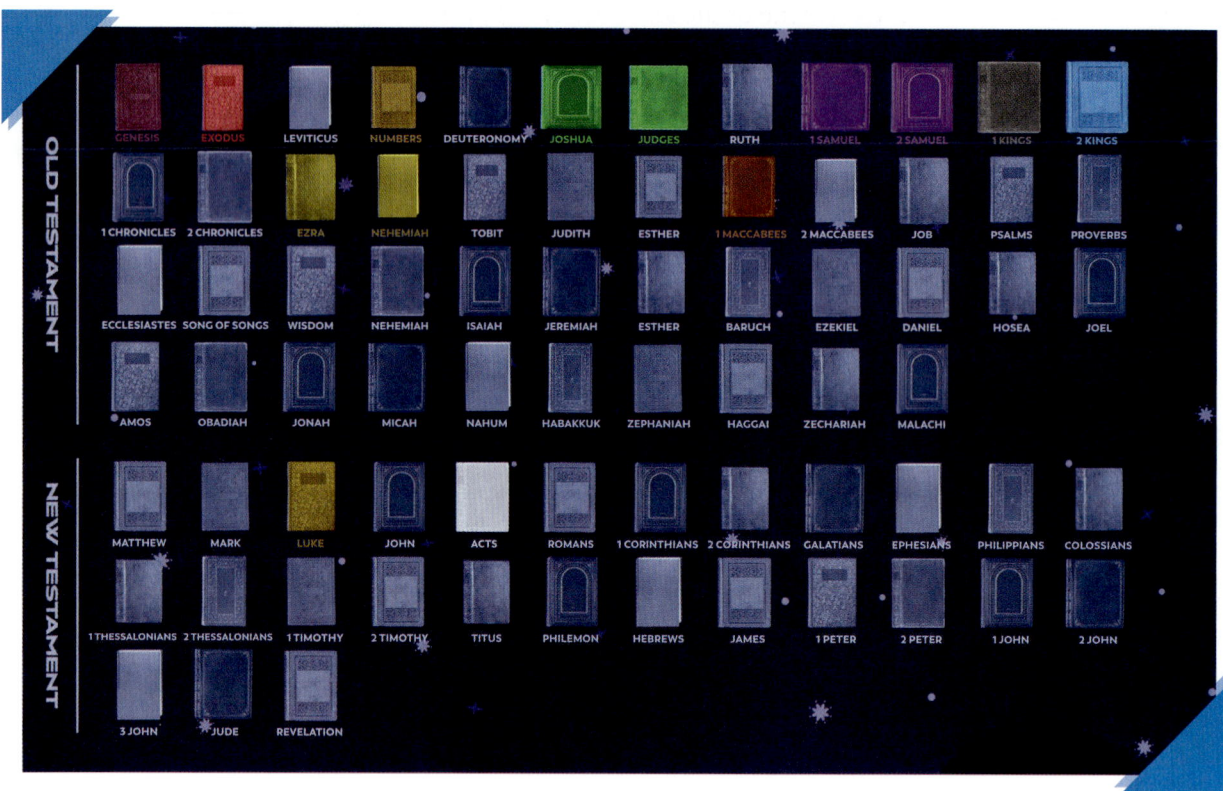

In *The Great Adventure* Bible Study Program, *The Bible Timeline* Learning System arranges the key people, places, and events of the Bible into twelve color-coded periods. The chart in the back pocket of this workbook uses the same system to show you how the books of the Bible fit together to tell the story of **SALVATION HISTORY**. *The Bible Timeline* teaches the "big picture" of the Bible and gives us the tools to really understand our story as God's people.

The twelve periods of *The Bible Timeline* are shown in the banner across the bottom of the page and on your timeline chart.

6 | ENCOUNTER

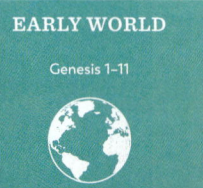
EARLY WORLD
Genesis 1–11

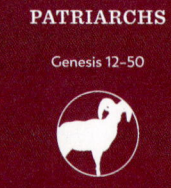
PATRIARCHS
Genesis 12–50

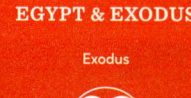
EGYPT & EXODUS
Exodus

DESERT WANDERINGS
Numbers

CONQUEST & JUDGES
Joshua, Judges,
1 Samuel 1–8

ROYAL KINGDOM
1 Samuel 9–31, 2 Samuel,
1 Kings 1–11

Look at your *Bible Timeline* chart to get familiar with the different periods. Notice especially where the books of the Bible appear on the chart and how the flow of people and events relates to those books.

You may already be familiar with some of the key events, like "The Flood" (Noah's ark), "David kills Goliath," and "Nativity of the Lord." Find those three stories on your chart. For each one, pay attention to the name of the time period, along with its color and dates. These will help you remember the stories later.

> "All Scripture is inspired by God."
> —2 Timothy 3:16

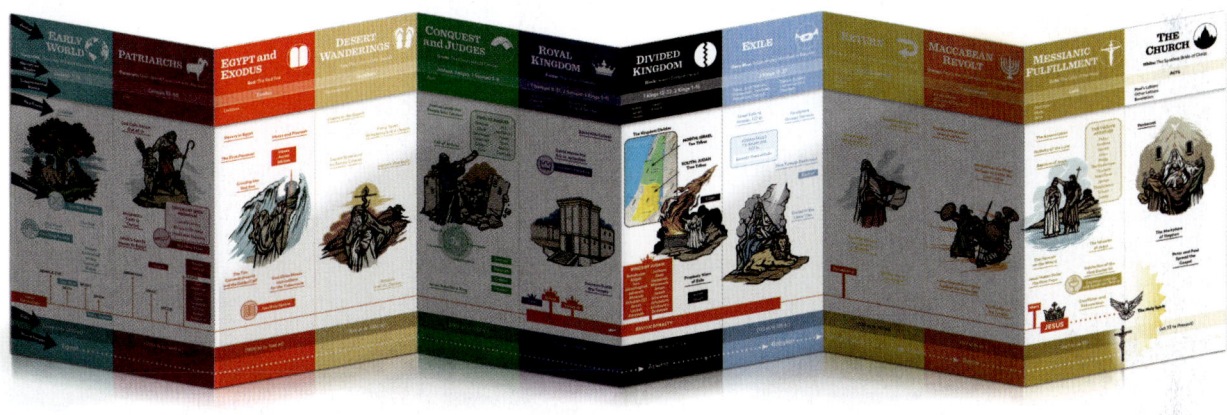

If You Ask Me

- Do you know some other Bible stories already? What Bible story has really stuck with you since you first learned it? What makes it so memorable?
- Which *Bible Timeline* period is already familiar to you? What do you know about it? Where did you learn about it?
- Which people in the Bible can you remember? What do you remember about them?

Lesson One – Introduction to the Bible | 7

Dive In Video

Introduction to the Bible . . . . Mark Hart

"Scripture is God's way of speaking directly to all of us." —Mark H.

DIVE IN

The **BIBLE** may look like one book, but it is actually a collection of seventy-three different books. These books were written over the course of thousands of years by many authors in many places. The books have different writing styles, purposes, audiences, and literary forms.

Sometimes **SACRED SCRIPTURE** describes certain events as they happened in history. Other times, symbols and creative writing are used to communicate the truth in other ways. Across this variety of books, remember:

- All of Scripture is the story of God's great love for his people throughout history. (The Bible is *about* God.)
- All of Scripture is the **INSPIRED** Word *of* God. (The Bible is God's own words.)
- All of Scripture is God's **REVELATION** to us. (The Bible is *from* God.)
- In all of Scripture, God is speaking personally to you, about you. (The Bible is *your* story, too.)

Sometimes people find the Bible confusing because it contains so many books and so many kinds of writing: histories, laws, poems and songs, love letters, wise sayings, visions, Gospels, and personal letters. God speaks to us through all these books. But how can we make sense of everything?

8 | ENCOUNTER

> **Scripture Is Like a Letter from God to You!**
>
> St. Gregory the Great was a pope a long time ago. We call him "the Great" because he was a wonderful leader, teacher, and writer. Gregory called the Scriptures "a letter from Almighty God to his creature"—a letter directly from God to me and you!

The *Encounter* program helps you make sense of the Bible by looking at the one big story that's woven through it: the story of **SALVATION**. The **OLD TESTAMENT** tells us how God made us to love him and how we turned away from him. It tells us how sin entered our lives and how much we need a savior. The **NEW TESTAMENT** tells us the story of our Savior, Jesus. It tells us about his life on earth two thousand years ago, his Resurrection from the dead, and the beginnings of his **CHURCH**. Together the Old and New Testaments tell us the story of salvation from the beginning of time until now.

Take another look at your *Bible Timeline* chart. Notice which narrative books are listed for each time period. In upcoming lessons, we'll focus on key events from these fourteen books that tell God's story and ours—the story of salvation.

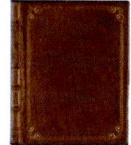

If You Ask Me

- Have you ever related to a book, movie, show, or song as if it were telling your own story or describing your own feelings, even though it was created by someone else? How did that make you feel?
- When have you felt inspired? What was the situation? Who or what inspired you? What were you inspired to notice, do, feel, or change?
- Who or what makes you think about God? Why?

Lesson One – Introduction to the Bible | 9

Got It

1. **How many books are there in the Bible?**

    a. 27

    b. 46

    c. 73

    d. 14

2. **How many books will we be focusing on in this program?**

    a. 27

    b. 46

    c. 72

    d. 14

3. **All of Scripture is _____ and is God's _____ to us. It is God's Word.**

    a. nice, nugget

    b. inspired, Revelation

    c. Revelation, inspiration

    d. wordy, puzzle

DIVE IN ACTIVITY

Bible Race

For this program, you need to know how to find your way around the Bible. The only way to get better is to practice—so let's do it! Below are several verses. Your leader will give a signal to begin the search for each. The first person to find and read the verse wins the round. May the fastest Bible searcher win!

- [ ] John 3:16
- [ ] Ephesians 4:24
- [ ] John 14:6
- [ ] Genesis 3:15
- [ ] Psalm 63:1
- [ ] Deuteronomy 17:18
- [ ] 1 Samuel 3:4
- [ ] 1 John 4:8
- [ ] John 4:8
- [ ] 1 Corinthians 13:13

Which verse got you thinking? Why? Write your answer here.

_____
_____
_____
_____
_____

BIBLICAL CHARACTER VIDEO

You! .... Fr. Frankie Cicero

"You are precious in my eyes, and honored, and I love you ... I am with you." —Isaiah 43:4–5

BIBLICAL CHARACTER PROFILE

You!

You may think the adventures of the Bible are ancient history. But the truth is that God calls people today. In fact, God is calling you. *You* are a main character in the epic story of God's love, just like the biblical characters you'll be meeting in *Encounter*. You have your own story, your personal adventure with God.

Fr. Frankie shared how, in the unexpected place of a grocery store, God called him to share the Good News with a woman who really needed it. His story reminds us that encounters with God happen anywhere, anytime, to everyone.

Since you were conceived, God has been writing your unique story—and even now, while you are in middle school, God is still writing. An amazing adventure with God awaits you. As we study God's Word, you will learn how to listen for God's invitation.

12 | ENCOUNTER

Sharing What You Love

God wants us to share our faith. In the Gospel of Matthew, Jesus gives his **APOSTLES**—and us!—a mission: to tell other people about him. He commands us to "go … and make disciples of all nations" (Matthew 28:19–20).

Fr. Frankie had an adventure—a chance to share his faith in an unexpected way in an unexpected place. We never know when God will give us an opportunity to tell someone else about him. Thinking about what to share helps us prepare for the opportunities God gives us.

What are three things about God and our **CATHOLIC** Faith that you think are worth sharing? Examples are knowing Jesus, the Mass, the Eucharist, Adoration, the Blessed Mother, the Rosary, *lectio divina* (praying with Scripture), works of mercy, grace before meals, praise and worship, youth group, retreats, Advent and Christmas, Lent and Easter, the saints, Gregorian chant, and on and on. Can you think of more? What is special to you? Write three things here:

1. _____

2. _____

3. _____

Now think about specifically where and how you could share these things with others. For example, "In the morning before school, I could tell my sister, 'I'm praying for you today.'" Or "I could tell my friend who is having a hard time, 'In my hard times, Jesus has always been there. He is here for you too!'"

_____

_____

_____

Living It Out

As we start the *Encounter* program, consider the three habits below that you can practice over the next weeks and months that will make the study more meaningful, powerful, and effective in your life. Are you ready for the challenge?

1. Commit to praying every day. This can be very simple. Think of a few specific ways you could pray daily.

2. Go to Mass every Sunday. Beforehand, go to the USCCB website (usccb.org), click on "Daily Readings," and read the Sunday Mass readings *before* Mass. This little habit will dramatically improve how much you remember from the readings. By the end of this program, you will also know much more about what these readings mean.

3. Talk to a friend about what you are learning, wondering, and thinking. It might be awkward at first, but talking about your faith helps both your faith and your friendships grow.

WORDPLAY

Apostle: From a Greek word meaning "one who is sent." The original twelve Apostles were chosen by Jesus to preach the Gospel and make disciples of all nations.

Bible: From the Greek word *biblia*, which means "collection of books." The Bible contains seventy-three books of many different types.

Catholic: A word meaning "universal"; the name for the Church instituted by Jesus and passed down through the successors of the Apostles.

Church (capital "C"): The whole assembly of believers in Jesus Christ throughout the world.

inspired: From a Latin word meaning "to breathe into," referring (for example) to how the Holy Spirit guided the human authors of the Bible as they wrote the truth God wants us to know for our salvation.

New Testament: The latter part of the Bible, which details the life, death, and Resurrection of Jesus Christ, along with the early history of his Church.

Old Testament: The first part of the Bible, which describes Creation, the Fall, and God's ongoing attempts to repair his relationship with humanity.

Revelation: Divine truth that God communicates to us through his Word (Scripture) and the teachings handed down to us (Tradition).

Sacred Scripture: The collection of ancient biblical texts that are inspired by God and reveal his nature and presence to his people.

salvation: Our deliverance, through Jesus Christ, from the powers of sin and death.

salvation history: God's redemptive plan in human history, culminating in Jesus Christ, who completely reveals the Father to us.

CLOSING PRAYER

"Thank you, Father, for the chance to discover more about the great story that we are a part of. Thank you for helping us see our own unique places in the story. Thank you for the community of faith that surrounds us and strengthens us. Help us to grow as we learn about your Word. In Jesus' name, we pray. Amen."

Lesson Two
Early World

EARLY WORLD　　　　　　　　　　　　　　　　　　　　　　GENESIS 1–11

16 | ENCOUNTER

The Big Picture

To fully experience any great story, we must start at the beginning. Whether it's the origin of a hero's superpowers, an epic love story, or the story of our own lives, the beginning is critical. This is especially true of the greatest story of all time: salvation history.

It's easy to settle for a vague sense of Genesis as a simple story about a man and a woman in a garden with a snake and some fig leaves—and then quickly move on. But the beginning—*our* beginning—goes far deeper than that. So, let's go deeper.

OPENING PRAYER

"Lord God, we ask you to draw us into our human story as we enter this lesson. Help us to understand more about how you made us, how sin hurt us, and how you enacted a plan for our salvation. May we see how the stories of the Bible are like our own stories. May we learn and grow from everything you reveal. In Jesus' name, we pray. Amen."

REMEMBER THIS!

"I will put enmity between you and the woman, and between your seed and her seed; he shall bruise your head, and you shall bruise his heel."

—Genesis 3:15

Genesis 3 tells the story of Adam and Eve, who are freshly created, enjoying bodies without any pain or imperfection. They are in Paradise. They are in love. They are living without shame in God's presence. It can be tough to believe that, just one chapter later—after a disastrous encounter with the serpent—Adam and Eve end up hiding behind fig leaves, ashamed, blaming each other for their failures, and facing the terrible consequences of sin.

Yet, even in the distressing confusion of sin, hope remains. Adam and Eve stumbled and suffered because of their disobedience, but God already has a plan to save them: he will give his only begotten Son. The "new Adam"—Jesus—will be born of the "new Eve"—Mary—who is the crown of creation. His sacrifice and her obedience will crush the serpent. (Notice what's under Mary's foot in the image on the right.)

God's plan and promise were at work from the very beginning. Genesis 3:15 is a verse for your heart because it declares that even when suffering and brokenness seem endless, God has a plan! Trust him.

The Immaculate Conception by Giovanni Battista Tiepolo

18 | ENCOUNTER

WARM UP

The Bible Timeline

Draw a line from each period on *The Bible Timeline* chart to its color and then to the meaning of the color:

Period	Color	What the Color Means
Early World	Tan	The green hills of Canaan
Patriarchs	Burgundy	The Spotless Bride of Christ
Egypt and Exodus	Green	The Red Sea
Desert Wanderings	White	Judah returning home to brighter days
Conquest & Judges	Gold	God's blood covenant with Abraham
Royal Kingdom	Black	The color of royalty
Divided Kingdom	Yellow	The color of the desert
Exile	Turquoise	Israel's darkest period
Return	Purple	Judah "singing the blues" in Babylon
Maccabean Revolt	Baby Blue	The color of Earth viewed from space
Messianic Fulfillment	Orange	Fire in the oil lamps in the purified Temple
The Church	Red	The gifts of the Magi

Lesson Two – Early World

TIME PERIOD OVERVIEW

Early World

Adam and Eve in the Garden of Eden by Johann Wenzel Peter

If you miss the beginning of a story, you might seriously misunderstand the rest. Here, we aren't talking about just any story. We are talking about *the* story: who God is, who we are, how we got here, what life means, and where we're headed. We want to get the beginning of this story right.

Remember that the Bible isn't trying to explain science or math or give a detailed history. The Bible is trying to reveal our true identity and purpose. Maybe you've looked at a family photo album that does something similar: it shows you where you came from, which helps you understand your place in a story that is bigger than you are. The Bible tells us the greatest story of all—and our personal stories have a place in it.

20 | ENCOUNTER

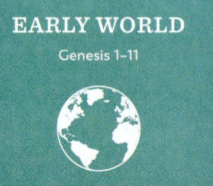
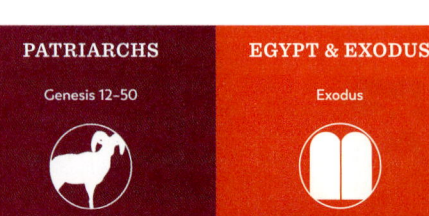

On your *Bible Timeline* chart, find the Early World panel (turquoise). Notice that the narrative book for the Early World is Genesis (the word means "beginning"). This lesson takes us into the book of Genesis and the beginning of our human family story. We will follow God's love as it brings everything in the universe into existence—including Adam and Eve, our first parents. We will also learn about the catastrophe of sin.

Genesis contains some wild stories: people who live for hundreds of years, a worldwide flood, murder, scandal, and more names than you could possibly remember. (Don't worry. The point isn't for you to remember them all.) Ultimately, the *Encounter* program wants to teach you about *your* story. A good look into Genesis can help you understand more about your past, your current experience, and even your family. (You think *you* have issues with your siblings? Wait until you meet Cain and Abel.) As you go deeper into the Bible, you will see your own joys and struggles reflected in the stories.

> "I praise you, for I am wondrously made. Wonderful are your works! You know me right well."
>
> —Psalm 139:14

If You Ask Me

- Genesis means "beginning." What are some important events in your own personal Genesis story? What has happened in your life up to today that has shaped who you are?

- Adam and Eve fell into temptation and chose sin. What modern temptations do you and your friends face? How can you resist temptation and avoid falling into sin?

- One of the big stories in the early world is about Cain and Abel. Cain allowed his feelings of jealousy to grow into hatred, and Abel became his target. Can you relate to either Cain or Abel? Have you ever been jealous of a sibling? Has anyone ever been jealous of you? Have you ever taken out your feelings on someone who had done nothing wrong? What can you learn from your experiences?

Lesson Two – Early World

DIVIDED KINGDOM	EXILE	RETURN	MACCABEAN REVOLT	MESSIANIC FULFILLMENT	THE CHURCH
1 Kings 12–22 2 Kings 1–16	2 Kings 17–25	Ezra Nehemiah	1 Maccabees	Luke	Acts

> **Early World** .... **Mark Hart**
>
> *DIVE IN VIDEO*
>
> *"When we go way back to the beginning, we see where we all come from. And we see that we're born out of love." —Mark H.*
>
> *During the video, Mark will ask you to pause and read two Bible stories. Find and mark them in your Bibles now so that you can open to them quickly when you need to:*
> - *Genesis 3:1–13, The Fall*
> - *Genesis 4:1–10, Cain and Abel*

In the beginning, there was nothing ... except God. There was no air, no space, no light, no creature of any kind. Only God existed, and he existed as the **TRINITY**—one God in three Persons: Father, Son, and Holy Spirit. Within the Trinity, the Father loves the Son, and the Son loves the Father. The fruit of their love is the Holy Spirit.

God's love always overflows. So, in the nothingness, God's love overflowed into Creation. He created light first, and then he continued to create. He made the day and the night, the sky, the land and the sea, the sun and the moon, the creatures of the sea and air, and the creatures of the land.

Then, at last, God made his greatest work: a man and a woman, in his image!

The Six Days of Creation*

GOD BRINGS FORM	GOD FILLS THE FORM
Day 1: light and dark	Day 4: sun, moon, stars
Day 2: water and sky	Day 5: fish and birds
Day 3: land (and plants)	Day 6: land animals, human beings

*Based on a table in *The Bible Timeline: The Story of Salvation*, by Jeff Cavins, Sarah Christmyer, and Tim Gray (West Chester, PA: Ascension, 2019), 19.

All creation came from God's goodness and shares in his goodness. "And God saw everything that he had made, and behold, it was very good" (Genesis 1:31). And then, at last, God rested—which is the reason we rest on Sunday, the Lord's Day.

The man and the woman were Adam and Eve, our first parents. God gave them a paradise, the **GARDEN OF EDEN**, as their home. Everything they needed and wanted was there, and they lived without shame or suffering, in close friendship with God and in harmony with each other.

God asked them not to eat the fruit of one tree: "Of the tree of the knowledge of good and evil you shall not eat, for in the day that you eat of it you shall die" (Genesis 2:17).

You'd think they could follow one simple rule, right? Not so much.

Satan, appearing as a cunning serpent, lied to Adam and Eve. He made them distrust God's love for them. Surrounded by God's goodness, you'd think they would ignore Satan's lies. But Adam and Eve faced what we all face: temptation. Sin seems attractive and can be hard to resist. We are tempted and tricked into doubting God's goodness and love. We are tricked with lies.

Adam and Eve disobeyed God and ate the fruit. Immediately, their sinful act filled them with guilt and shame. For the first time ever, they wanted to hide from God. When God asked them what happened, Adam blamed Eve and Eve blamed the serpent.

Lesson Two – Early World | 23

Adam and Eve had to leave Paradise. They would now experience pain, struggle, suffering, and death. But why did God make them leave? Did God stop loving them? Was he punishing them?

No. Think of a parent telling a child not to touch a hot stove. If the child touches the stove anyway and is burned, the burns are not a punishment but a consequence. Similarly, it wasn't that God no longer loved Adam and Eve. Of course he loved them. But their sin had wounded them and made them afraid, distrustful, and disobedient. It had robbed them of the original justice and holiness they'd had when God created them. That is why this event is called **THE FALL**, because Adam and Eve fell away from the grace of God. Without that, they couldn't live in Paradise. It was impossible.

Adam and Eve passed on the wound of sin to their children and to everyone who came after them. Their sin is called **ORIGINAL SIN**, and it affected all creation. Because of it, we have all inherited a condition of sin, which we call the fallen state. We see its effects every day in the way we drift toward sin.

We were created in God's image, but because of Original Sin, our desire for what is good and true is weak. We go crooked when we mean to go straight. We prefer a lie to the truth. The Church has a big word for this tendency to sin: **CONCUPISCENCE**. It's the way we imagine sin to be easy and fun—easier and more fun than doing what is truly good for us and for others. It's the way we want to rely on ourselves rather than on God.

From Genesis 4 on, we see the terrible damage concupiscence causes: lies, jealousy, betrayal, and murder. But we also see hope. God promises Adam and Eve that he will send a savior one day. And while the world waits for its **SAVIOR**, we will meet Abel and Abraham, Moses and Miriam, David and Esther, and many others—good people who show us that all is not lost for humanity.

We Are Made in God's Image

"So God created man in his own image, in the image of God he created him; male and female he created them. And God blessed them, and God said to them, 'Be fruitful and multiply, and fill the earth and subdue it; and have dominion over the fish of the sea and over the birds of the air and over every living thing that moves upon the earth. ... And God saw everything that he had made, and behold, it was very good.'"

—Genesis 1:27–28, 31

If You Ask Me

- List some details that stand out to you from the Creation story in Genesis. Why do you think those details stay with you? What about them is important to you?
- Can you think of a time when you gave in to a temptation that had negative consequences? What was that like?
- Has a consequence ever helped you in the long run? What did you learn from it?

Lesson Two – Early World | 25

Got It?

1. **Human beings arrived on the _____ day of creation.**

    a. sixth

    b. fifth

    c. first

    d. seventh

2. **God asked Adam and Eve not to eat the fruit to _____.**

    a. control and limit them

    b. show his power over everything

    c. protect them

    d. test whether they were good

3. **Sin tricks us into _____.**

    a. doubting God's love

    b. thinking we know better than God what is good for us

    c. doubting God's goodness

    d. all of the above

DIVE IN ACTIVITY

Sketch

Choose one of the key events that Mark talked about ("Creation"; "The Fall"; "Cain and Abel") and draw a picture of yourself in it. Or draw yourself in a scene from another story in Genesis if you know one, such as naming the animals with Adam (Genesis 2:18–20), helping Noah load the ark (Genesis 7:1–10), or building the Tower of Babel (Genesis 11:1–9).

Don't worry about how well you can draw (stick figures are welcome!) but be prepared to talk about your sketch.

- **The event (and Bible verses) you chose:**

- **Why you chose this event:**

- **How it relates to you:**

- **What do you think we should learn from it?**

Abel. . . . . Tanner Kalina

"The Lord had regard for Abel and his offering, but for Cain and his offering he had no regard." —Genesis 4:4–5

BIBLICAL CHARACTER PROFILE

Cain and Abel

Tanner shared his experience of competing to be the starting shortstop on the varsity baseball team. He and his competitor were equal in skill and ability in almost every way except for one thing: Tanner was the first on and last off the field. He was passionate about playing. He was hungry for victory and excellence. He was all in.

Tanner's story gives us insight into Cain and Abel, the brothers in Genesis 4. Abel offers God the firstlings of his flock, including "the fatty portions"—the most delicious parts—while Cain offers God just a portion of his harvest. God accepts Abel's offering, but not Cain's.

Is the point that God has food preferences? No. The Bible doesn't tell us exactly why Abel's sacrifice is more pleasing to God, but it suggests that Abel gives God his best, while Cain does not. Abel gives from his heart. He does not hold back. He is invested, dialed in, and committed.

God challenged Cain to give more of himself, saying, "If you do well, will you not be accepted?" (Genesis 4:7). But instead of trying to do better, Cain gave in to his anger and jealousy and murdered his brother.

Remember that the Bible teaches us a lot about our own stories. You probably aren't a shepherd like Abel. You may or may not play baseball like Tanner. But you have the same choice: to give with passion or to do only the minimum. This choice is most important in your relationship with God, but it also matters at school, at home, and everywhere else.

Abel shows us what God really wants from us: our hearts. Are we giving God our best? Are we really showing up for our family and friends? Let's live, pray, and really invest ourselves in self-offering like Abel.

All In

Find Cain and Abel on your *Bible Timeline* chart, and then read their story in **Genesis 4:1–16**.

Tanner's baseball story—which is really about Abel's sacrifice—reminds us that God wants us to be all in. He wants us to give from our hearts. It can be tempting to do the minimum in school, in sports, in our activities, and in our faith. But you're made for more than the minimum.

In what areas of your faith can you commit to going all in? Maybe you can pay better attention at Sunday Mass. Maybe you can offer a certain prayer as soon as you wake up. Maybe you can commit to going to Confession once a month. What are three things you can do to really go all in?

1. _____

2. _____

3. _____

The Flood.................................Genesis 6–9

People Scattered at the Tower of Babel........Genesis 11:1–9

Find Out More

Early World

Your *Bible Timeline* chart mentions two more Early World stories, which you might know already: the story of Noah's ark ("The Flood") and a story about what happened when people tried to build a tower to heaven.

Living It Out

The stories of Adam and Eve and of Cain and Abel show us what sin looked like from the very beginning. Sin is a trick and a lie every time. If we want to be truly free and happy, we must avoid sin. When we sin, we can ask God to heal us and help us do better in the future.

- At bedtime, examine your conscience for the day. Think about the day: what you did, what you said, the interactions you had with others. Is there anything good from the day that you wish to offer back to God in thanksgiving? Is there anything you should not have done or could have done better? Be honest with yourself and ask God to help you tomorrow.

- Go to Confession. This sacrament is truly amazing: God never gets tired of forgiving us when we go to him. If you are nervous, ask a family member or friend to go with you. In Confession, through the sacrament of the priesthood, you are talking to the priest who is representing Jesus—and Jesus is thrilled that you are there! (To help yourself prepare for Confession, you can use the **Examination of Conscience for Middle School** in the back of your workbook, starting on p. 138.)

- Sharing our lives makes us stronger in faith. Ask a family member or friend to be your faith partner. Once a week, talk about how you're doing in your faith life.

WORDPLAY

concupiscence: The desire or inclination to commit sin.

Fall, the: The event in Genesis when Adam and Eve disobeyed God and "fell" from grace.

Garden of Eden: Also called "Paradise." God made this special place for Adam and Eve to live in before the Fall.

Original Sin: The "stain" of sin we inherited from Adam and Eve, which means we are born in a "state of sin" and require redemption.

Savior: Jesus Christ, the one who delivers us from the consequences of sin and death.

Trinity: The three distinct Persons who make up the single divine nature of God: the Father, the Son, and the Holy Spirit.

CLOSING PRAYER

"Lord God, we see our story in the story of Genesis. From the beginning, you loved us and wanted to be with us. When we chose sin, you still loved us and opened the way back to you. Help us to see how our own story is in the story of Scripture. As we study your Word, show us how to grow, trust, and make our way back to you. Open our eyes and ears to see and hear what you want to reveal. In Jesus' name, we pray. Amen."

Lesson Three
Patriarchs – Egypt

| PATRIARCHS | GENESIS 12–50 |

| EGYPT | EXODUS 1–3 |

The Big Picture

God is truth, so he never lies. He honors his covenants. He never breaks his promises. But his timing doesn't always fit our desires or expectations. We often look for an instant result, not realizing that God usually plays the long game when carrying out his work. He always comes through—but it's on his perfect timetable, not ours.

And sometimes God makes really interesting choices in forming his team. He picks the least likely players and still wins, every single time. He levels up with old game controllers. He creates masterpieces with broken crayons.

OPENING PRAYER

"Lord God, from the beginning you took our broken world and broken hearts into your fatherly heart and worked wonders. You drew a family together, slowly mended their brokenness, and worked through even their worst mistakes and failures. As we learn the story of your people, show us how you want to do the same in our personal stories. Give us great trust, open hearts, and belief in your promise. In Jesus' name, we pray. Amen."

REMEMBER THIS!

"By you all the families of the earth shall bless themselves."

—Genesis 12:3

These words are God's first promise to Abram. God also promised to give Abram and his wife, Sarai, many descendants, even though they were already old—too old to have children. God gave them new names to confirm his promise. To Abram he gave the name Abraham, meaning "father of many nations," and to Sarai he gave the name Sarah, meaning "mother of many nations." Over many generations, God fulfilled all his promises to them.

34 | ENCOUNTER

WARM UP

Coats

Later in today's lesson, you will learn about Joseph. When Joseph was young, his father gave him an amazing, colorful coat as a sign of how much he loved him.

Imagine that God gave you a wonderful coat as a sign of your special relationship with him.

In real life, God hasn't given you a coat, but he has given you personal traits and talents that show his love for you. His gifts make you unique and unrepeatable. Using the prompts below, write down your personal talents and traits on the stripes of the coat, and then color it with your favorite colors.

1. Your nickname or another affectionate name you've been called
2. An activity you are good at and feel confident doing
3. A special talent you have
4. A chore you enjoy doing
5. A superpower you would like to have
6. A song you like
7. A place you'd love to go
8. A sport or game you enjoy

Lesson Three – Patriarchs – Egypt

TIME PERIOD OVERVIEW

Patriarchs and Egypt

Abraham's Journey from Ur to Canaan by Jozsef Molnar

Look on your *Bible Timeline* chart and find the **Patriarchs** period (burgundy) and Egypt, the first part of the **Egypt and Exodus** period (red). The narrative books for these periods are Genesis and Exodus.

These periods show how God gathered a people to himself and freed them so they could know him and **WORSHIP** him. It begins with a **COVENANT** that God made with Abraham. In his covenants, God promises to be with us. He reminds us that he isn't just watching us from far away without caring. Covenants are God's solemn promises that unite us with him, as a family. Sometimes they include promises we make to him.

36 | ENCOUNTER

EARLY WORLD	PATRIARCHS	EGYPT & EXODUS	DESERT WANDERINGS	CONQUEST & JUDGES	ROYAL KINGDOM
Genesis 1–11	Genesis 12–50	Exodus	Numbers	Joshua, Judges, 1 Samuel 1–8	1 Samuel 9–31, 2 Samuel, 1 Kings 1–11

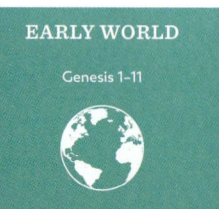

What a story! A very old man without any children leaves his own people and makes a dangerous journey to the land of Canaan (hundreds of miles away!) to settle among strangers. Why? Because God asks him to. Abraham trusts God, and he trusts God's promises: land, more descendants than there are stars, and the blessing of all the families on earth.

The covenant passed from Abraham to his son Isaac, and then to his grandson Jacob. One night when Jacob was grown, he wrestled with an angel. They wrestled all night, and in the morning God changed his name to Israel ("wrestled with God") and blessed him. Jacob became the father of the twelve tribes of Israel.

These men—Abraham, Isaac, and Jacob—are known as the **PATRIARCHS**. They are the father figures of both **JEWS** (also called **ISRAELITES**) and **CHRISTIANS**.

One of Jacob's sons was Joseph, whose beautiful coat we mentioned earlier. Joseph's brothers sold him into slavery (really!). But after many adventures, Joseph became a powerful figure in Egypt. He forgave his brothers, and he brought them and their families to live in Egypt during a famine, where they had plenty of food.

Later, another Egyptian pharaoh enslaved Joseph's descendants. Now they were trapped in a land that wasn't their own among people who worshiped false gods. They had lost their identity, their community, and their friendship with God. That's when God called Moses to lead them out of Egypt to freedom, to the land he had promised Abraham: the **PROMISED LAND**.

The story is really about God's plan and God's initiative. You'll notice that Abraham's adventures weren't Abraham's idea; Joseph's adventures weren't Joseph's idea; Moses' adventures weren't his idea, either. Their adventures were God's idea. God chose Abraham, Joseph, and Moses for *his* plan: to bless his people there, here, and ultimately, through the Church, everywhere in the world.

If You Ask Me

- Who are the patriarchs and matriarchs in your family? What do you know about your grandparents (or great-grandparents and generations beyond)? Are any of your ancestors from places far away from where you live now?
- What are your family's most important places? Where does your family gather for important moments, vacations, or traditions? What do you like about these places?

Lesson Three – Patriarchs – Egypt | 37

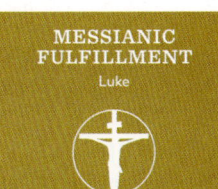

DIVIDED KINGDOM	EXILE	RETURN	MACCABEAN REVOLT	MESSIANIC FULFILLMENT	THE CHURCH
1 Kings 12–22 2 Kings 1–16	2 Kings 17–25	Ezra Nehemiah	1 Maccabees	Luke	Acts

Dive In Video

Patriarchs and Egypt . . . . Mark Hart

"Taking revenge is easy. ... Rising above all that to show mercy, that's true strength." —Mark H.

During the video, Mark will ask you to pause and read two Bible stories. Find and mark them in your Bibles now so that you can open to them quickly when you need to:
- *Genesis 45:1–10, Joseph Makes Himself Known to His Brothers*
- *Exodus 3:2–14, Moses and the Burning Bush*

DIVE IN

The Patriarchs, whose stories aren't so different from our own, were part of a greater plan that was ultimately fulfilled in Jesus. We've seen how, over time, God was making himself known to more and more people—first to Adam and Eve; later to Abraham, Isaac, and Jacob; and then to the families of Jacob's sons, the twelve tribes of Israel.

A family tree helps us keep the story straight. One of God's promises to Abraham was that he would have more descendants than there are stars in the sky. Look at Abraham's family tree on pages 40–41. You can see already how it grows with each generation. Notice especially the long row of Jacob's twelve sons. All of them, except Reuben and Joseph, became heads of the tribes (Reuben lost his share, and Joseph received a double share that went to his two sons, Ephraim and Manasseh). The twelve tribes were named for Jacob's sons or grandsons: Simeon, Levi, Judah, Dan, Naphtali, Gad, Asher, Issachar, Zebulun, Benjamin, Ephraim, and Manasseh.

Notice too, below them, that Moses, Aaron, and Miriam are Levites, members of the priestly tribe of Levi's descendants.

> *"You shall be my people, and I will be your God."*
> *—Jeremiah 30:22*

REUBEN SIMEON LEVI JUDAH DAN NAPHTALI GAD ASHER ISSACHAR ZEBULON JOSEPH BENJAMIN

JACOB
(ISRAEL)

In the Gospels, Matthew traces Jesus' ancestry back to Abraham. Luke traces it even further, all the way back to Adam. Don't worry about memorizing every detail or branch on that tree. Just become familiar with the overall picture so that you can follow the greater plan.

The family tree helps us visualize the key figures in Mark's tour through the time periods so we can see how God began fulfilling his promises to Abraham in a growing family. It also helps us see how, when the Israelites became enslaved in Egypt, God set in motion the plan for their freedom.

If You Ask Me

- Names are important to God. As Mark says, that's where a relationship starts—with learning someone's name. Why do you think God changed the names of Abraham, Sarah, and Israel? What does your name mean?
- Think about God's promise to give Abraham many descendants. How does the family tree above show how God fulfilled it?
- Remember that all events of salvation history ultimately lead to Jesus. What traits does Moses have in common with Jesus?

Lesson Three – Patriarchs – Egypt | 39

ABRAHAM'S FAMILY TREE

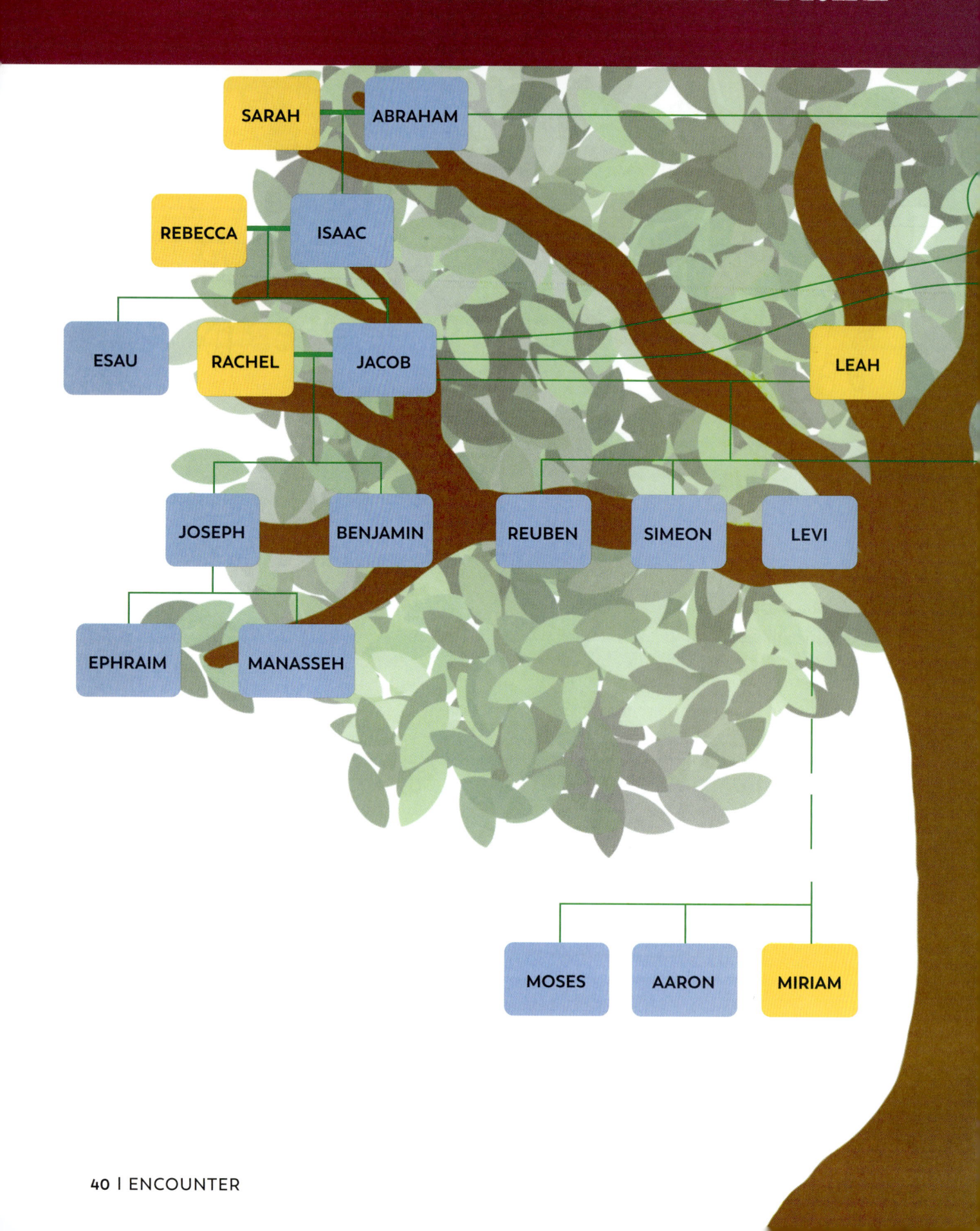

- SARAH — ABRAHAM
  - REBECCA — ISAAC
    - ESAU
    - RACHEL — JACOB — LEAH
      - JOSEPH
        - EPHRAIM
        - MANASSEH
      - BENJAMIN
      - REUBEN
      - SIMEON
      - LEVI
        - MOSES
        - AARON
        - MIRIAM

40 | ENCOUNTER

HAGAR

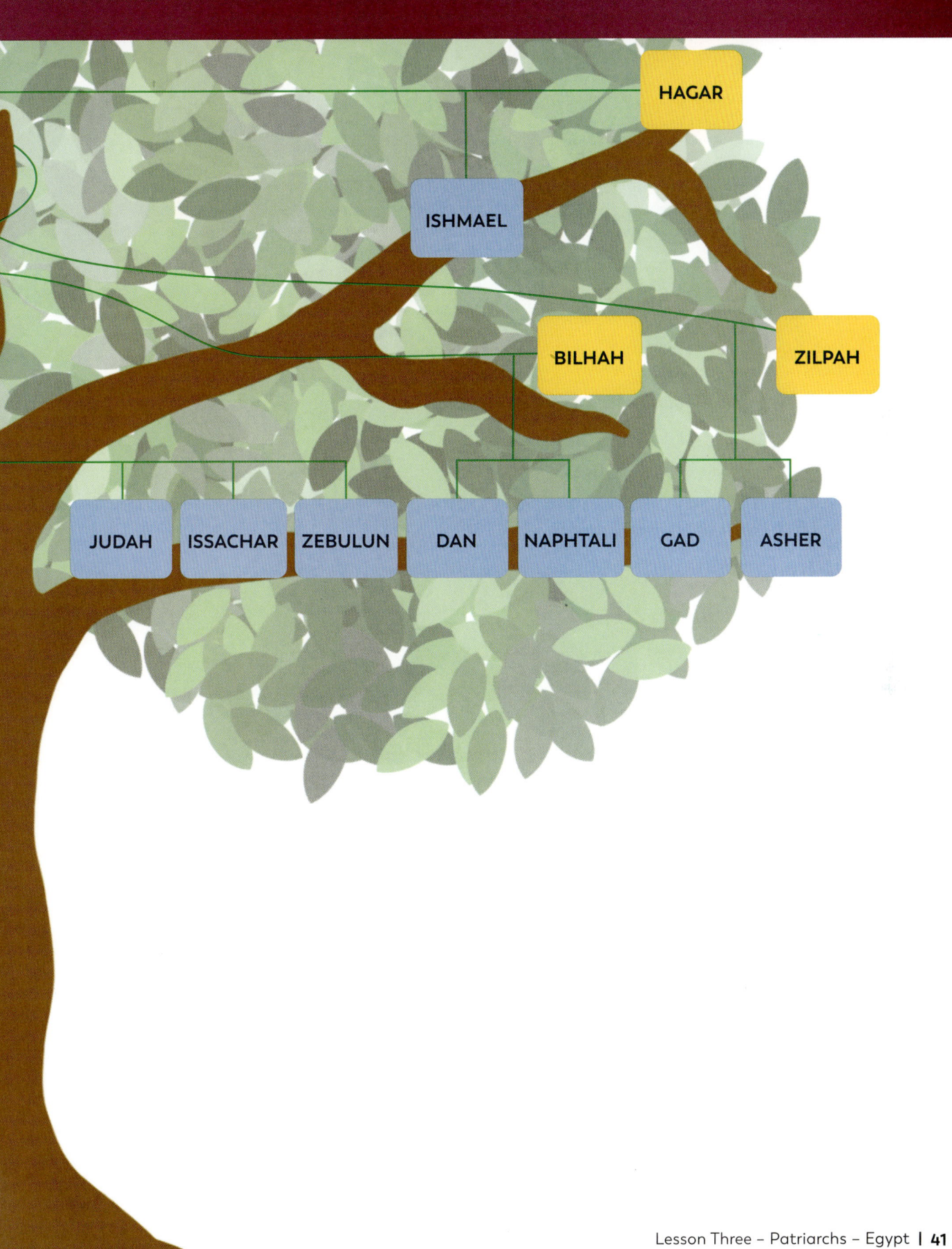

ISHMAEL

BILHAH

ZILPAH

JUDAH | ISSACHAR | ZEBULUN | DAN | NAPHTALI | GAD | ASHER

Lesson Three – Patriarchs – Egypt | 41

Got It?

1. **A patriarch is _____.**

    a. a priest

    b. a father figure or leader of a family or tribe

    c. a prophet

2. **Abraham, Isaac, and Jacob are the ancestors of _____.**

    a. everyone in the world

    b. Matthew and Luke, the Gospel writers

    c. Jesus

3. **The family tree of Genesis is not just a family history. It also shows the history of _____.**

    a. God's plan to save us

    b. the Egyptian pyramids

    c. the whole ancient world

DIVE IN ACTIVITY

Promise

Choose a verse from Genesis that you find meaningful—
one of the verses below or another that strikes you:

- Genesis 1:1
- Genesis 1:27
- Genesis 4:6-7
- Genesis 50:20
- Genesis 1:3-4
- Genesis 1:31
- Genesis 12:3

How does the verse you chose remind you of God's love and promise? Write your verse below and then decorate it. If you like, take a picture of it, print it, and hang it where you can see it every day.

Verse:

BIBLICAL CHARACTER VIDEO

Miriam . . . . Ashley Hinojosa

"And Miriam sang to them." —Exodus 15:21

BIBLICAL CHARACTER PROFILE

Miriam

Ashley Hinojosa struggled with comparing herself to her older brother. He had more friends than she did, played multiple instruments, and was always first chair in the band. Ashley was in the band, too, but she was never first chair. Because he was older, he got to sit in the front seat of the car and was invited to do things that she couldn't. He seemed to know more, do more, and get noticed more.

Comparing herself to her brother was always a source of disappointment and insecurity for Ashley. But then she discovered that the points of comparison weren't the full truth about who she was or her abilities. She came to see that she was special in her own ways.

Enter Miriam the prophet. Miriam was the sister of two men with great callings—Moses and Aaron—but she is introduced in Exodus 15 as a prophet in her own right.

We don't know many details of Miriam's life, but her story is her own. After the Israelites crossed the Red Sea on dry land, Miriam led all the Israelite women in thanksgiving and song. We know that she later had

44 | ENCOUNTER

leprosy but was cured of it, and she died before the Israelites reached the Promised Land.

Miriam's story reminds us to stop comparing ourselves to other people. Sometimes we think we're better than someone else; on the flip side, we often think we don't measure up. Either way, the comparison steals our joy and sense of belonging.

So, who are you? What are you being called to do? You won't discover the answers by comparing yourself to others. Only by listening to God's voice and answering his call can you discover who you really are in his eyes.

Loved, Not Compared

Find Miriam on your *Bible Timeline* chart. Which period is she in? Now read about her in **Exodus 15:19–21**.

Comparing ourselves to others usually makes us feel bad about ourselves and blocks us from seeing the wonderful way God has made us. Remember that when God looks at you, he doesn't compare you to another person. He loves you for being *you*.

Ask your family and friends to name several things they love about you, then write down their responses below. You will begin to get just a glimpse into God's great love for you.

_____

_____

_____

_____

_____

_____

God Calls Abram out of Ur.	GENESIS 12:1–7
Jacob Steals His Brother's Blessing.	GENESIS 27:1–39
Joseph's Brothers Sell Him into Slavery	GENESIS 37:12–36
Joseph Saves the Egyptians from Famine	GENESIS 41:46–49, 53–57
Joseph Forgives His Brothers	GENESIS 50:15–21
Moses in the Bulrushes.	EXODUS 1:15–2:10

Find Out More

Patriarchs and **Egypt**

Here are more stories about the Patriarchs, and one story that you might know already about Moses when he was a baby.

Living It Out

As you have seen, the theme of family is huge in God's plan. God the Father uses our human families to teach us about his love and about our identity as his sons and daughters.

- Choose one family member to pray for with special focus. At the beginning of the week, ask for the intentions of the person you've chosen and say that you will be offering prayers and sacrifices for them this week. Set reminders for yourself to follow through on praying for this family member's intentions.

  After a week (or a few days if your family is very large), move on to another family member until you have covered everyone.

- Each day, do one helpful or kind thing for another family member without being asked. Maybe you can put away laundry for someone else. Maybe you can bring someone a drink or snack. Maybe you can take out the trash. Maybe you can create a card or drawing that says how much you love and appreciate the other person. Maybe you can serve another person's plate before yours at lunch or dinner.

WORDPLAY

Christians: A follower of Christ who has been baptized in his name.

covenant: From a Latin word meaning "to agree on." More than a contract, a covenant is an exchange of persons that helps establish an ongoing relationship.

Israelites: The descendants of the Patriarch Jacob (whose other name was Israel). Jacob's twelve sons were the ancestors of the twelve tribes of Israel.

Jews: Another name for the Israelite people, or "men of Judah," used in the period of the Exile and after.

patriarch: The male head of a family or tribe, often the eldest or most respected man in the family. A **matriarch** is the female head of a family or tribe.

Promised Land: The region that God promised to give to Abraham and his descendants as an inheritance.

worship: To honor or show reverence to God alone.

CLOSING PRAYER

"Thank you, God, for being our good and loving Father. Thank you for always doing what is best for us and for always keeping your promises. Help us to know you better as a father. Help us to see one another as sisters and brothers. Give us patience with our family members and help us grow in love together. In Jesus' name, we pray. Amen."

Lesson Four
Exodus – Desert Wanderings – Conquest & Judges

Exodus — Exodus 4–40

Desert Wanderings — Numbers

Conquest & Judges — Joshua, Judges, 1 Samuel 1–8

The Big Picture

A home, an identity, a community, a quest, an adventure, freedom: we are made for these. And these are what God gives his people in the books of Exodus, Numbers, and Joshua. As slaves in Egypt, the Israelites had lost their true identity, their community, and their close relationship with God. But through Moses, God has freed them. Now God will give them a new covenant—to bring them to the Promised Land—and he gives them his commandments to protect their freedom. Only as a free people can they come to know him again, worship him, and finally find their home.

OPENING PRAYER

"Lord God, our liberator, you call us out of the slavery of sin into freedom. You call us to leave behind the ways of thinking and acting that lead to misery. You call us into a life of joy as your people. Show us how we, like the Israelites, are on a journey from captivity to the place you have prepared for us. Help us listen to your voice and to grow daily along the way. In Jesus' name, we pray. Amen."

REMEMBER THIS!

"I am the Lord your God, who brought you out of the land of Egypt, out of the house of bondage. You shall have no other gods before me."

—Exodus 20:2–3

The First Commandment might seem obvious. God is God, right? But the Israelites needed this commandment because they had been so immersed in Egyptian beliefs that they had lost sight of God himself, the one true God. In fact, it was very hard for them to separate themselves from what they'd known in Egypt, and they kept returning to the worship of false gods even after God showed them his power, rescued them from slavery, and gave them this commandment.

Few of us have actual pagan statues on our nightstands. But we should ask ourselves: Is God first in our hearts and lives, or do we allow other things to come before him? Who, or what, do we actually place on the throne of our hearts?

WARM UP

The Ten Commandments

Working from your memory (don't look up anything yet!),
unscramble the words of the Ten Commandments:

1. I am the Lord your God; you shall not have *enrstga dsgo* before me. _____

2. You shall not take the *amne* of the Lord your God *ni ivan*. _____

3. Remember to keep holy the *'sodLr yDa*. _____

4. Honor your *rathef dan thermo*. _____

5. You shall not *likl*. _____

6. You shall not commit *ludertay*. _____

7. You shall not *alest*. _____

8. You shall not bear *sealf newtiss* against your *rbgeohin*. _____

9. You shall not covet your neighbor's *fiwe*. _____

10. You shall not covet your neighbor's *odgos*. _____

TIME PERIOD OVERVIEW

Exodus, Desert Wanderings, Conquest & Judges

Have a look at your *Bible Timeline* chart. Today we'll cover a lot of ground with the Israelites—from **Exodus (red)** through **Desert Wanderings (tan)** and into the Promised Land in **Conquest & Judges (green)**.

When God's people were enslaved in Egypt, God chose Moses to set them free. Moses cooperated with God's call. He went to Pharaoh and demanded that he let the Israelite people go. It was a dangerous, difficult mission. Pharaoh was the ruler of an empire, a powerful king, like a god himself—so why should he listen to this scruffy messenger? He refused.

Because of Pharaoh's refusal, the Egyptians suffered ten **PLAGUES**. Each of the plagues represented one of the false gods that the Egyptians worshiped. God showed that he was the true God by defeating the Egyptian gods one by one.

Before the tenth and final plague, God warned Moses that all the firstborn in the land of Egypt would die. He told the Israelites to sacrifice a lamb and use its blood to mark the doorposts of their homes. That evening, the Israelites ate the lamb with their shoes on and their belongings ready to go. Then, at midnight, all the firstborn in Egypt died—except for the Israelites, whose houses were marked with the

52 | ENCOUNTER

EARLY WORLD	PATRIARCHS	EGYPT & EXODUS	DESERT WANDERINGS	CONQUEST & JUDGES	ROYAL KINGDOM
Genesis 1–11	Genesis 12–50	Exodus	Numbers	Joshua, Judges, 1 Samuel 1–8	1 Samuel 9–31, 2 Samuel, 1 Kings 1–11

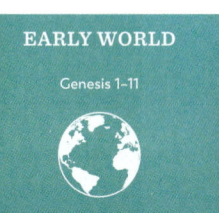

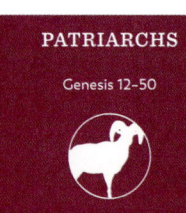

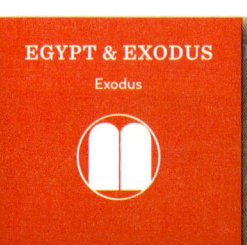

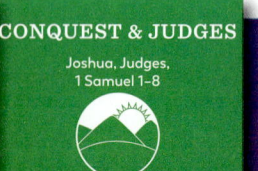

blood of the lamb. This was the first **PASSOVER**, because when God came down to take the firstborn, he saw the blood and "passed over" those houses.

After the tenth plague, Pharaoh finally relented, and the Israelites fled from Egypt. But Pharaoh quickly changed his mind. He sent the Egyptian army to chase the Israelites into the sea and be destroyed. But through Moses, God saved his people again; he divided the sea so they could walk across on dry land, with walls of water on either side. Pharaoh and his army were the ones who were destroyed in their pride and rage. The Israelites passed through the water into freedom—freedom in the desert.

The Israelites were free, but they were not ready to go into the land that God had promised to Abraham. They disobeyed and complained. They still had Egypt's false gods in their hearts and minds.

God used their time in the desert to turn their hearts to him. He performed miracles to feed them—bread from heaven, quails, and water from a rock. Most importantly, God established a covenant with Moses and all the Israelites. In it, he gave Moses the **TEN COMMANDMENTS** and the whole Law (the Torah), and he promised to make the Israelites his own people (see Exodus 19:5–6).

God also gave the people detailed instructions for building the Tabernacle and the beautiful Ark of the Covenant. The **TABERNACLE**, or tent of the covenant, was where God dwelt. Inside was the **ARK OF THE COVENANT**, the golden chest that held the stone tablets with the Ten Commandments. On the lid of the Ark was the mercy seat, the throne where God's presence rested.

After forty years, the people were ready. Moses died, and Joshua led them into the Promised Land. Miraculously, they crossed the Jordan River on dry land, just as they had crossed the Red Sea forty years before.

Now came the time of conquest. With God leading them, the Israelites conquered their enemies and divided the land among the twelve tribes. God's people were finally home, in the land God had promised to Abraham.

If You Ask Me

- Who are the most powerful people in our society? What makes them powerful? Which individuals can you think of who use their power and authority for good?
- The Israelites were enslaved for generations in Egypt. What are we "enslaved" to today? What do we allow to control our time and focus?
- When do you find it hard to obey the people you should obey, like parents and teachers? What happens when you do not obey them?

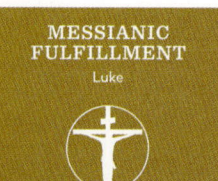

Dive In Video

Exodus, Desert Wanderings, Conquest & Judges . . . . Mark Hart

"Guardrails help guide us in the right direction and keep us safe. And that's what the commandments do. They guide us in the right direction. They keep us safe." —Mark H.

During the video, Mark will ask you to pause and read two Bible stories. Find and mark them in your Bibles now so that you can open to them quickly when you need to:
- *Exodus 32:1–6, The Golden Calf*
- *Joshua 3:8–17, The Israelites Cross the Jordan on Dry Land*

DIVE IN

Freedom from slavery! A dramatic, miraculous rescue! Did the Israelites rejoice and trust God with grateful hearts?

Not for long. The desert was vast, hot, and dry. There were no comfortable homes and little food. The Israelites quickly began to complain about God and doubt his plan. This was not a new problem. While they were still enslaved in Egypt, they had also doubted God. Many had even worshiped the false Egyptian gods.

In the desert, God provided for them, but they complained at every point. When they were hungry, he gave them **MANNA** (bread from heaven) and wild quail. They moaned because it wasn't the food they were used to. When they were thirsty, God made water spring out of desert rocks. They groaned that it wasn't cold enough. Sometimes they even grumbled aloud that they wished they had never left Egypt!

> **God's Name**
>
> In the video, Mark talks about the burning bush, where God appeared to Moses and asked him to lead his people to freedom. Moses asked God to tell him his name that day, and God said his name is "**I AM WHO I AM**" (Exodus 3:14). God's name is so holy that the people would not speak it aloud. They called God *Adonai* (which means "LORD") instead.

54 | ENCOUNTER

God gave the Israelites the Ten Commandments at Mount Sinai to protect them and show them how to worship him and live together peacefully. But the people almost immediately broke the commandments; they even made a golden calf to worship as a new god! Their disobedience and their stony hearts kept them wandering for forty years.

What does this story about the Israelites thousands of years ago have to do with you? You didn't melt down your family's jewelry to create a false idol, but you've probably struggled with putting other things before God. You may not moan about having to eat manna, but you might complain instead of being grateful for God's constant gifts. On a bad day, you too might have doubted that God has an amazing plan for you.

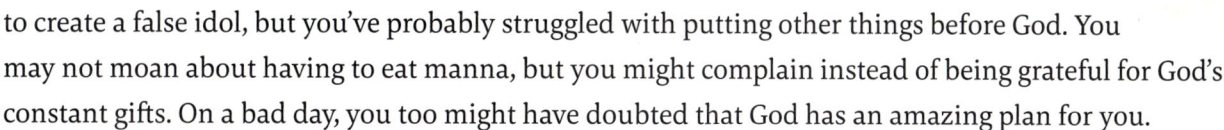

We sometimes behave like the whining Israelites in the desert. But God keeps calling us back to him, showing his love for us, drawing us back to his commandments so we can enter heaven—the Promised Land that he has prepared for us.

The Great Commandment

"Hear, O Israel: The Lord our God is one Lord; and you shall love the Lord your God with all your heart, and with all your soul, and with all your might."

—Deuteronomy 6:4–5

Moses Receiving the Ten Commandments by Gebhard Fugel

As the Israelites settled into the Promised Land, the period of **Judges** began. God wanted his people to be different from other nations and set apart. He didn't want them to worship false gods and celebrate sinful behavior. He gave them commandments that taught them to live differently, and he gave them judges instead of a king to guide them.

The Israelite **JUDGES** weren't like our judges today, who decide in court how laws should be applied. These judges were leaders or champions, often good warriors, who were chosen by God to deliver the people from their enemies. But the Israelites didn't want judges. They begged God for a king so they could be more like their neighbors, who all had kings to rule over them.

Maybe you can relate. Have your parents ever said no when you wanted something everyone else seemed to have or when you wanted to do something everyone else seemed to be doing? Maybe you argued with them, but your parents were firm in setting a different standard for you. Your parents do this because they want what is best for you. That is also why God set boundaries for the Israelites.

But, as you'll see in the next lesson, when the Israelites finally got what they wanted and had kings, they found even more trouble.

If You Ask Me

- What is something your family does differently than everyone else? Why does your family have this different standard? How do you feel about it?
- What is something you see everyone else doing or having that you don't think is good or healthy? What problems do you think this thing causes? What is a different, better choice?
- Why do you think it is so hard for the Israelites to trust God, even though they experience miracles and his divine intervention? What causes them to constantly drift away from trusting God's goodness?

Gratitude Notes

I'm grateful for
Example:
my dog, Spot

I'm grateful for

I'm grateful for

I'm grateful for

I'm grateful for

I'm grateful for

I'm grateful for

I'm grateful for

I'm grateful for

I'm grateful for

I'm grateful for

I'm grateful for

Got It?

1. **The Israelites sinned and broke the Ten Commandments by _____.**

    a. writing a new set of commandments

    b. making a golden calf statue that they worshiped

    c. going back to Egypt

    d. stealing from other groups they met

2. **For _____ years, the Israelites wandered in the desert because they were not yet ready for the Promised Land.**

    a. 5

    b. 25

    c. 40

    d. 100

3. **When they were settled in the Promised Land, the Israelites were ruled by _____ instead of kings like other nations.**

    a. prophets

    b. pharaohs

    c. priests

    d. judges

DIVE IN ACTIVITY

Grumbling and Gratitude

Like the Israelites, we all struggle with our own grumbling. God wants to help us become grateful and to trust in his goodness.

Think about the things or people you often grumble about: chores, homework, rules, a neighbor. What else can you think of? Be specific and write them down. Then, focus on one or two of them and think about them again. Is there something about that situation or person that you can be grateful for instead? Is there something important about them that you've been missing?

What do I grumble about?	What is something about the situation or person that I can be grateful for instead?
Example: Setting the table for dinner.	All of us get to be together at dinner. I get to help out. I get to make things a little easier for Mom and Dad.

Lesson Four – Exodus – Desert Wanderings – Conquest & Judges

BIBLICAL CHARACTER VIDEO

Gideon . . . . **Tanner Kalina**

"And [Gideon] said to him, 'Please, Lord, how can I deliver Israel? Behold, my clan is the weakest in Manasseh, and I am the least in my family.'" —Judges 6:15

BIBLICAL CHARACTER PROFILE

Gideon

In high school, Tanner struggled with self-confidence. Then one day, the school counselors asked him to lead a small group on an upcoming retreat. At first, Tanner didn't want to do it because he didn't think he had what it took. Him? Talking about Jesus and being a role model? But the counselors persuaded him, and Tanner ended up leading the retreat group. To his surprise, it went so well that some of the other students named Tanner's leadership as a highlight of the whole retreat.

Gideon was also insecure and uncertain when God called him. Gideon also questioned his own ability. After all, he came from the lowest clan and was the least important member of his own family. But God called Gideon, instructing him to do bold things—like destroying a false temple and fighting the huge Midianite army with just three hundred men. Even though Gideon was afraid and unsure, he followed and obeyed God. And he triumphed.

God is calling you, too. Maybe you're thinking, "Why me? Doesn't God know that I'm not as smart or holy as my friends?" or "What if people think I'm weird?" or "What if God asks me to do something I'm afraid to do?"

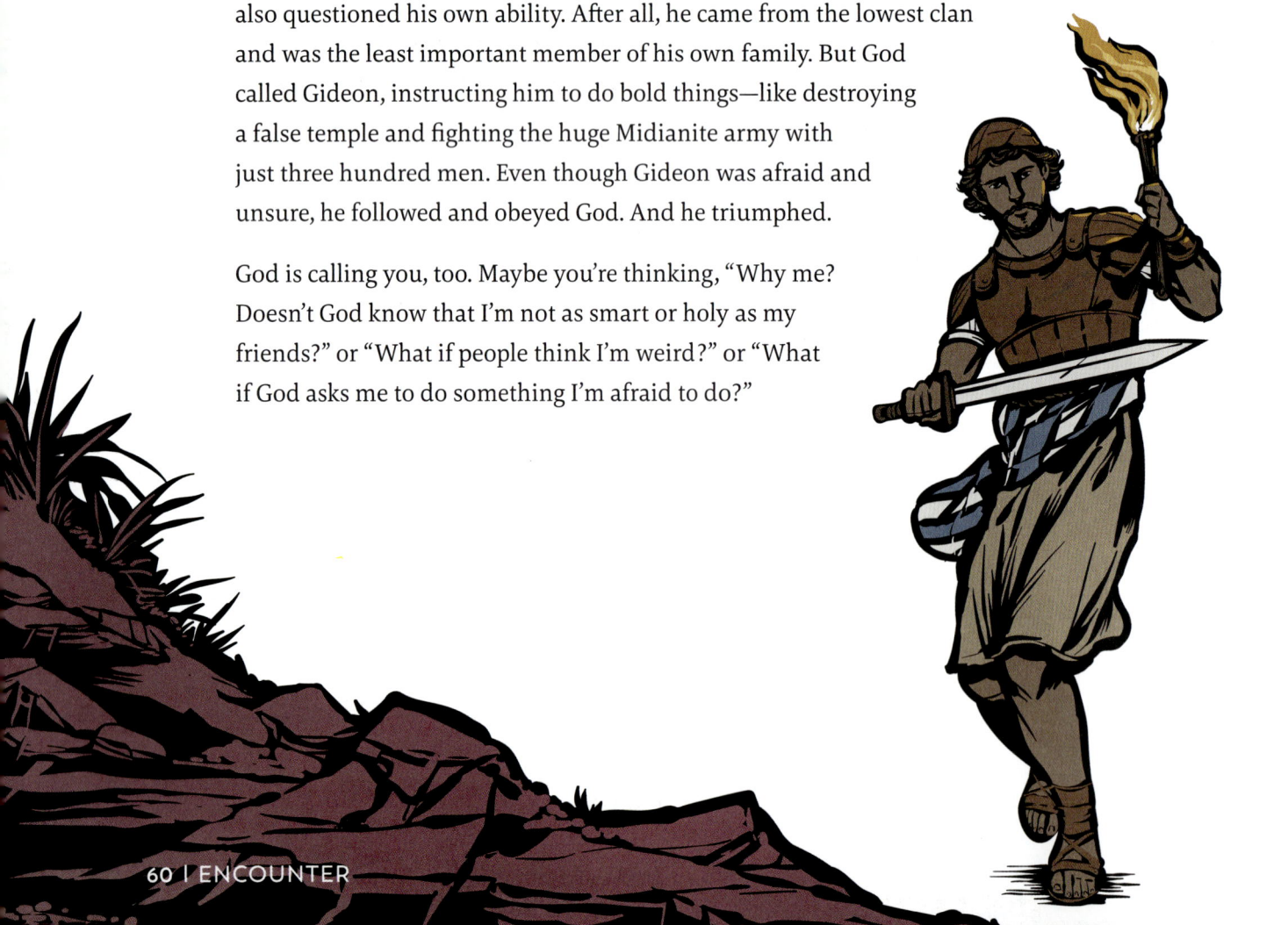

You—yes, you!—are called to be a saint. God wants to use you to show others more about him. Remember, God doesn't call the equipped; he equips the called. The Lord invites you to say yes to a mission that only you can do. God knows you even better than you know yourself, so you can trust him even if you're unsure or afraid.

God worked through Tanner and Gideon, and he will work through you! Go forward with confidence and strength.

"I Will Be with You"

Find Gideon on your *Bible Timeline* chart. Which period is he in? Now read the beginning of his story in **Judges 6:11–16**.

Gideon was considered one of the mightiest judges of Israel. His story reminds us that when God asks us to do something, he gives us what we need to do it.

- Have you ever succeeded at something you didn't think you were good at? What was it?
- How did it turn out? How did you feel afterward?
- Is there anything in your life right now that you won't do because you think you won't be good at it? What is it? Do you think God might be nudging you to try?

Manna in the Desert	Exodus 16:14–21
The Israelites Build the Ark of the Covenant	Exodus 25:10–22
Twelve Spies Sent to Survey Canaan	Numbers 13:1–14:9
Balaam and His Talking Donkey	Numbers 22:21–35
Joshua Leads the People into Canaan	Joshua 3:14–17
The Fall of Jericho	Joshua 6:12–17

Find Out More

Exodus, Desert Wanderings, Conquest & Judges

Here are stories you can read to learn more about what happened to the Israelites from the time they left Egypt until they settled in Canaan.

Living It Out

Does your life show that God is number one? When others interact with you, can they see how important God is to you?

- Make an effort to practice your faith at all times. Go to Mass even when you're on vacation (check masstimes.org to find Masses wherever you are). Pray grace before every meal, including in public at school or in restaurants. This small choice shows that we recognize God's constant providence and that we place him first.

- Choose a short favorite prayer or Scripture verse to offer as soon as you wake up every morning. Consider putting your prayer or verse where you'll see it as soon as you open your eyes. No matter how briefly, pray first every day.

- Add some Christian music to your playlists. Have fun exploring all the different styles of Christian music. When these songs queue up, they will remind you to think about God and his goodness throughout the day.

WORDPLAY

Ark of the Covenant: The wooden, gold-covered chest that held the two stone tablets of the Ten Commandments and other sacred objects of the Israelites.

I AM WHO I AM: The holy name of God, first spoken to Moses. "I AM" or "I AM WHO I AM" is the English translation of the four-letter Hebrew word YHWH (commonly pronounced "Yahweh").

judges: The twelve leaders of Israel who were chosen by God to help defend the Israelites from their enemies.

manna: The heavenly food that God gave the Israelites while they wandered in the desert. Manna was white and sweet and could be made into cakes.

Passover: The Jewish feast that commemorates the night when God "passed over" the Israelite homes in Egypt, protecting their children from death and freeing them from slavery.

plagues: A series of devastating catastrophes that fell upon the Egyptians after Pharaoh refused to let the Israelites go and worship God.

Tabernacle: The portable tent that the Israelites used for worship in the desert. It housed the Ark of the Covenant.

Ten Commandments: Ten laws that God gave to the Israelites to teach them how to live and worship as a free people.

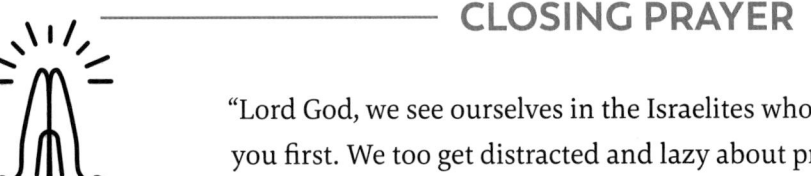

CLOSING PRAYER

"Lord God, we see ourselves in the Israelites who struggled to keep you first. We too get distracted and lazy about prayer and weak in our trust. We too put other things before you in our hearts. Give us the grace to see your goodness all around us, every day. When we are afraid to trust you, give us courage. Thank you for your patient love that always allows us to try again. In Jesus' name, we pray. Amen."

Lesson Five
Royal Kingdom – Divided Kingdom

Royal Kingdom — 1 Samuel 9–31, 2 Samuel, 1 Kings 1–11

Divided Kingdom — 1 Kings 12–22, 2 Kings 1–16

64 | ENCOUNTER

The Big Picture

Who is the king of your heart? That's an important question. It can also be a tough question. In the previous lesson, we saw how the Israelites still clung to Egyptian idols and false gods in the desert, despite everything God had done to provide for them. Later, during the time of the judges, they began to clamor for an earthly king.

The Israelites' story teaches us that, just as we shouldn't rely on false idols, we shouldn't put all our trust in princes or kings. We will see how Israelites learned this reality the hard way. There can be good earthly leaders, of course, such as King David—but even King David was great only when he acted as a man after God's heart. God must be our ultimate king—or, like the kingdom of Israel, our hearts will be divided.

OPENING PRAYER

"God our King, we place our full trust in you. Thank you for the men and women who serve as leaders and who remind us of your kingship. Help them always to follow you as the ultimate king. Help us always to serve you first, to be dedicated to serving you, and to give you honor and obedience. Long live Christ, our Eternal King! In Jesus' name, we pray. Amen."

REMEMBER THIS!

> "The Lord reigns; he is robed in majesty!"
>
> —Psalm 93:1

Salvation history is about God's relationship with his Chosen People and reveals his saving actions to deliver them from sin. Both in our own lives and across human history, we see a constant struggle to put God first. But when we pray and praise God, we proclaim that God is first, the King of the universe and of our hearts. Praise and prayer can be short, simple, and easy to remember, just like this verse. The Lord reigns!

WARM UP

Good to Be King

It would be good to be king, right? Kings live in fancy palaces. They have the power to command people to do things for them. They have the wealth to buy anything they could imagine. Being a king may seem like a good thing—but kings also have to *be* good. Being a good king is a huge responsibility: a kingdom comes with many people to provide for and protect.

What are the top five character traits that a king or queen needs in order to be a good, faithful, and strong ruler?

1.

2.

3.

4.

5.

Lesson Five – Royal Kingdom – Divided Kingdom | 67

TIME PERIOD OVERVIEW

Royal Kingdom and Divided Kingdom

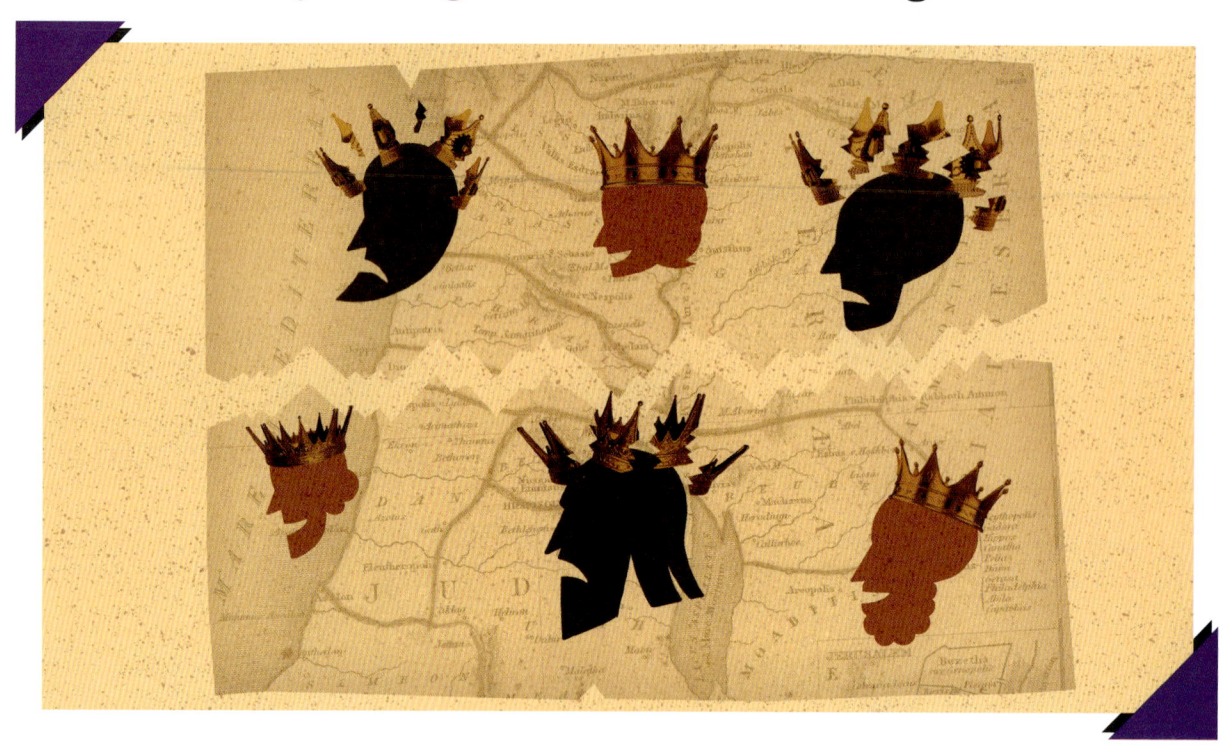

In the last lesson, the Israelites finally reached the Promised Land. They conquered their enemies, and each tribe settled into its own region. The people were led by their judges, but they wanted a human king.

On your *Bible Timeline* chart, find the **Royal Kingdom** (purple) and **Divided Kingdom** (black) panels. Notice which books tell these stories—1 and 2 Samuel and 1 and 2 Kings. Also, notice the names with crowns along the red bar at the bottom of those panels. Those are some of the Israelite kings.

The Israelites were a vast people now, a nation formed from the twelve ever-growing tribes. But they were not like other nations, and they were not meant to live like other nations. God called them

68 | ENCOUNTER

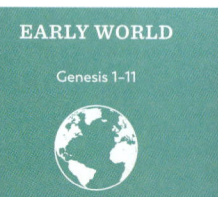

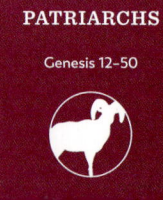

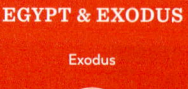

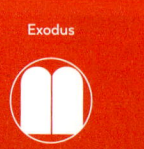

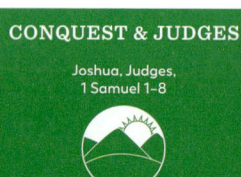

EARLY WORLD	PATRIARCHS	EGYPT & EXODUS	DESERT WANDERINGS	CONQUEST & JUDGES	ROYAL KINGDOM
Genesis 1–11	Genesis 12–50	Exodus	Numbers	Joshua, Judges, 1 Samuel 1–8	1 Samuel 9–31, 2 Samuel, 1 Kings 1–11

specifically to be his people, set apart. But they wanted to be like everyone else. They wanted to be led by an earthly king, just like most other nations at that time.

What they didn't realize was how the kings of other nations sent people's sons to war, heavily taxed the people, and often oppressed them. Samuel, Israel's last judge, warned the people that having a king would lead to trouble, but they insisted on having their own way. So, Israel received its first king.

In this lesson, we will look at four of Israel's kings:

- Saul (1 Samuel 9–31)
- David (1 and 2 Samuel)
- Solomon (1 Kings 1–11 and 2 Chronicles 1–9)
- Josiah (2 Kings 22–23 and 2 Chronicles 34–35)

After Solomon, the kingdom split into two parts: the Northern Kingdom (Israel) and the Southern Kingdom (Judah). Other kings followed; most of them were bad, and the two kingdoms grew weaker and weaker.

But God never wastes anything, not even our mistakes. He used these kings to foreshadow our salvation. The flashes of greatness in King David and King Solomon gave the people a glimpse of God's ultimate plan. In time, the Father would give his Son, the promised **MESSIAH**, to reign as King over all creation and conquer death itself.

If You Ask Me

- Why do you think the Israelites struggled so much with wanting to be like everyone else? How does this same problem affect our own lives?
- Jesus is not the ruler of a government or nation, but he is the King of the kingdom of heaven. How is he different from earthly kings? How does he use his power and authority?

Lesson Five – Royal Kingdom – Divided Kingdom | 69

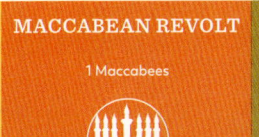

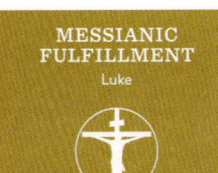

DIVIDED KINGDOM	EXILE	RETURN	MACCABEAN REVOLT	MESSIANIC FULFILLMENT	THE CHURCH
1 Kings 12–22 2 Kings 1–16	2 Kings 17–25	Ezra Nehemiah	1 Maccabees	Luke	Acts

Dive In Video

Royal Kingdom and Divided Kingdom . . . . Mark Hart

"God doesn't see from the outside in. He sees from the inside out. The Lord looks at your heart." —Mark H.

During the video, Mark will ask you to pause and read two Bible stories. Find and mark them in your Bibles now so that you can open to them quickly when you need to:
- *1 Samuel 16:7, 10–13, Samuel Anoints David*
- *2 Kings 23:2–3, King Josiah Renews the Covenant*

DIVE IN

King Saul united the kingdom, and King David made it larger and stronger. King Solomon enriched it and built the glorious Temple in the city of Jerusalem (the kingdom's capital). Later, King Josiah renewed the people's commitment to God.

Samuel **ANOINTED** Saul to be Israel's first king. The king was meant to rule by obeying the commandments and listening to leaders like Samuel who spoke for God. Saul began well; he united the kingdom and defeated its enemies. But then he grew resentful, vain, and jealous. He lost his trust in God and was no longer fit to lead God's people.

The next king was David, a handsome shepherd and brave warrior. David's heart delighted in God, and he became a sign to the people of God's own kingship. Best of all, God promised David that the Messiah would come from his family and establish a kingdom that would last forever.

A Man After God's Own Heart

"[God] raised up David to be their king; of whom he testified and said, 'I have found in David, the Son of Jesse, a man after my heart, who will do all my will.' Of this man's posterity God has brought to Israel a Savior, Jesus, as he promised."

—Acts 13:22–23

70 | ENCOUNTER

> "Then Solomon said ... 'I have built you an exalted house, a place for you to dwell in for ever.'"
> —1 Kings 8:12–13

After David came King Solomon, David's son, who built the magnificent Temple in Jerusalem. It became the center of worship for the whole nation of Israel. Inside was the Ark of the Covenant, the precious vessel that supported the mercy seat, where God's presence dwelt, and contained the Israelites' most sacred objects. (Remember the desert? Back then, the people had carried the Ark of the Covenant wherever they went.)

SOLOMON'S TEMPLE

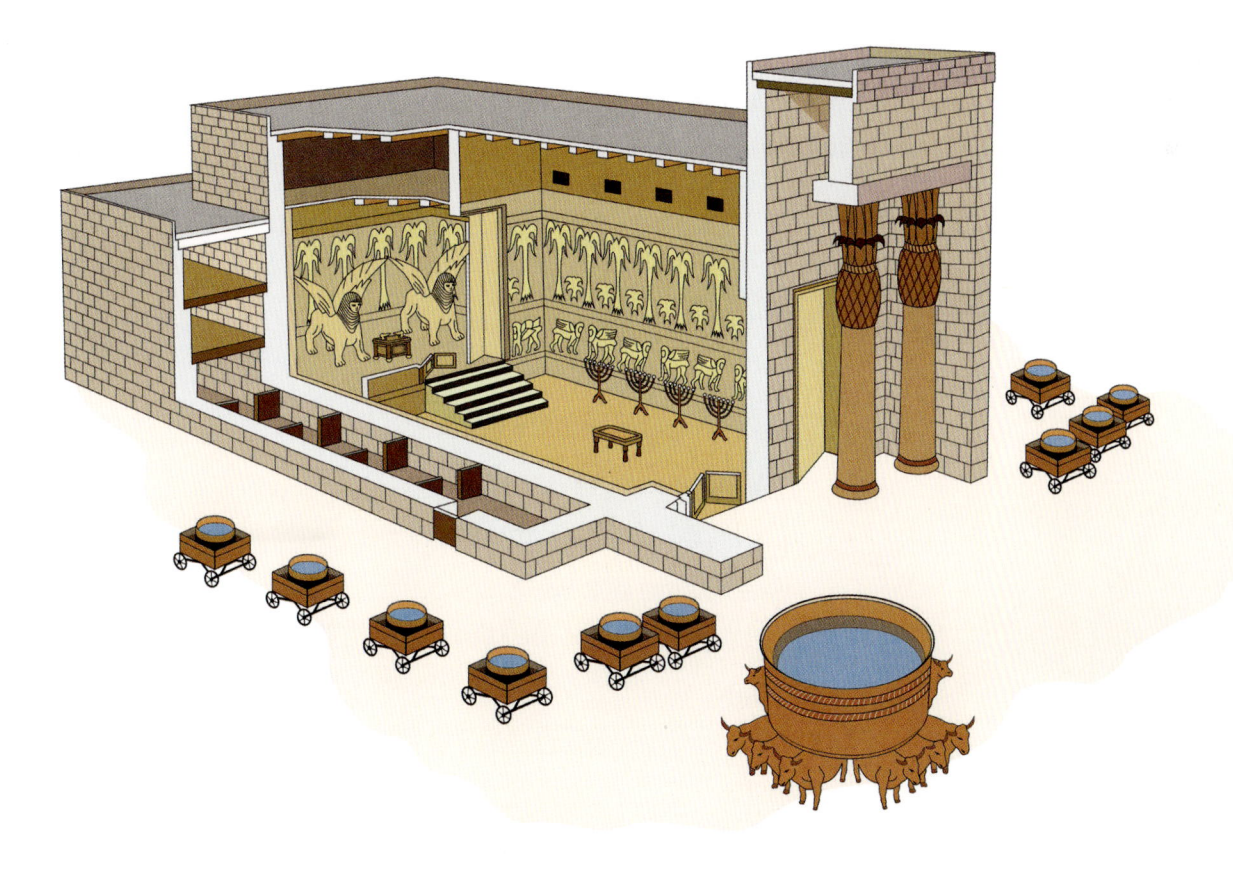

Under the reign of Solomon's son Rehoboam, the kingdom split into two hostile kingdoms—which made them easy prey for conquering armies. But one of the good kings after the split was young King Josiah of Judah, who was crowned when he was only eight. When he was older, he restored Temple worship and renewed the people's commitment to God's commandments.

Look at the graphics on this page and the next page to keep track of who's who. See what you can learn from each.

King: Saul
Strengths: Started strong by leading God's people into battle
Weaknesses: Grew prideful and vain and lost his way. Followed his own will, not God's.
Known for: Being Israel's first king but failing to trust God and obey him.
King-size truth: Don't forget who you really are, what your mission is, and that God is God. You can be happy and successful only if you put God's will first.

King: David
Strengths: "A man after God's heart." Deep personal faith. Repented with his whole heart after major sins.
Weaknesses: Fell into sin and temptation.
Known for: Slaying a huge giant, loving God, being a great king, writing many psalms, singing.
King-sized truth: Trust in the Lord and turn your heart to him constantly.

72 | ENCOUNTER

King: Solomon

Strengths: A wise and understanding heart. He built and dedicated the Temple in Jerusalem.

Weaknesses: His heart grew away from God. He taxed the people too heavily.

Known for: His wisdom, composing the Song of Songs, expanding and enriching the kingdom.

King-sized truth: Ask God for the grace and heart that you need to finish strong (Solomon didn't).

King: Josiah

Strengths: Being a good king even though his father and grandfather were awful kings. Initiating many religious reforms.

Weaknesses: He received a warning from God against fighting the king of Egypt, but he fought him anyway and was killed.

Known for: Recommitting to the covenant, reforming Judah.

King-sized truth: Turn your heart to God and his law, even if those around you don't.

If You Ask Me

- Of the four kings we've talked about, who is your favorite? What do you like about this person?
- How did God's warning about the Israelites having a king come true?
- Why do you think so many kings started well but ended up turning away from God?

Lesson Five – Royal Kingdom – Divided Kingdom | 73

Got It?

Each line below describes one of these kings. Use each king twice.

a. Saul   b. David   c. Solomon   d. Josiah

1. The first king of Israel   _____

2. A shepherd   _____

3. Built the Temple   _____

4. Had a father and grandfather who were bad kings   _____

5. Rediscovered the Law and committed his heart   _____

6. Sinned big time, but then repented   _____

7. Asked God for wisdom   _____

8. Was rejected by God for following his own will, not God's.   _____

DIVE IN ACTIVITY

Songs for the Lord

King David wrote the psalms as songs. The psalms were sung to music that was played on the harp or lyre.

Think of a line or a couple of lines from one of your favorite songs. Choose lines that remind you of God's goodness, his love, or something related to your faith.

What about these lines reminds you of God? Share your reflections with the group if you like.

_____
_____
_____
_____
_____
_____

BIBLICAL CHARACTER VIDEO

David .... Fr. Frankie Cicero

"Then David said to the Philistine, 'You come to me with a sword and with a spear and with a javelin; but I come to you in the name of the Lord of hosts, the God of the armies of Israel, whom you have defied.'" —1 Samuel 17:45

BIBLICAL CHARACTER PROFILE

David

When Fr. Frankie was 13 years old, he went to Bible camp. As he got on the bus to depart, one of the leaders invited him to share his testimony to the group later. Fr. Frankie was terrified! What would he say? What if people laughed at him? What if he sounded stupid? These fears were like the giant Goliath in his head. As he faced his fears, Fr. Frankie was like **David**.

David's brothers were all warriors, but David was a shepherd. While his brothers were off fighting the Philistines, David was at home, caring for his aging father, Jesse, and tending the family's sheep. One day Jesse asked David to deliver food to his brothers in the army camp.

When he arrived at their camp, David found the Israelite army being terrorized by Goliath, the giant. No soldier had the courage to fight Goliath, so the giant continued to taunt and threaten them. David had no military training, no armor, no heavy sword, and no weapons other than a sling. But he had complete confidence that God was with him, and he volunteered to fight Goliath himself. David's trust in God allowed God's power to work through him. The shepherd defeated the giant.

Fr. Frankie was scared to give his testimony, but he prayed and asked God to be with him. God provided: Fr. Frankie

76 | ENCOUNTER

went from clinging to his notes to tearing them up and throwing them away. His fears vanished and he delivered his testimony with confidence. Fr. Frankie's trust in God allowed God to touch others through his testimony.

You have the same God on your side! God wants to work powerfully through you. God is with you, and when you stay faithful in walking with him, you will slay giants. When you walk with God, you never walk alone.

Slaying Goliath

Find David on your *Bible Timeline* chart. What period did he live in? Now read the story of David and Goliath in **1 Samuel 17:1–50**.

In your own life, what "Goliath" do you need to slay? Your giant is probably not a literal enemy soldier, but it may be fear, insecurity, self-doubt, anxiety, or even a bad habit. A Goliath can be any problem that seems impossible to solve. Fr. Frankie shared how, with God's help, he faced his Goliath of fear and self-doubt and rose to the occasion.

Write a short reflection about a Goliath in your life. How does this Goliath affect your life negatively? What do you wish was different? Ask God to help you conquer your Goliath. Share your reflection with the group.

_____
_____
_____
_____
_____
_____

David Moves the Ark to Jerusalem . . . . 2 Samuel 6:1–5

Solomon Builds the Temple . . . . . . .1 Kings 6:1, 7, 11–13, 21–28, 38

Elijah on Mount Carmel . . . . 1 Kings 18:20–39

The Prophet Jonah and the Big Fish . . . . Jonah 1–2

Find Out More

Royal Kingdom and Divided Kingdom

Here are some stories you can read about the times when the Israelites had a king.

Living It Out

Is Jesus the true king of your heart? Did you know that by your **BAPTISM**, you also share in Jesus' royalty? You are a son or daughter of the King of Kings! Here are some ideas to help you begin living up to your royal calling:

- Write a brief prayer to Jesus as the king of your heart. Display it where you will see it and pray it often. Consider inviting your family to join you in this daily prayer.

- Jesus shows us that a true king reigns by serving others. This week, commit to doing one act of service each day. It may be something you do directly for your family or friends, like volunteering for extra chores or helpful tasks. It may be something small or even unknown by others, like saving someone a seat or saying a prayer for someone's intentions. It may even be something you do for a stranger or for the community, like picking up trash on the sidewalk when you pass by.

- The Church's teaching on **MORALITY** in the *Catechism of the Catholic Church* begins with St. Leo's words: "Christian, recognize your dignity" (CCC 1691). Understanding your own dignity as God's son or daughter is essential to your life in the Church.

  This week, try to build up your dignity and the dignity of others. Maybe you can be extra polite and courteous to others and avoid humor that makes fun of others. Maybe you can limit negative thoughts and statements about yourself and your body. Maybe you can respond to your parents the first time they ask you to do something instead of dragging your feet. You could dress nicely for Mass. You could pay more attention when someone is talking to you. If you look closely, you will find many ways to build up dignity in your ordinary day.

WORDPLAY

anoint: From a Latin word meaning "to smear with oil." Anointing is a ceremonial practice in which holy oil is smeared on someone as a sign that they are set apart for a special purpose.

Baptism: From a Greek word meaning "to immerse." Through Baptism, we become a new creation, an adopted son or daughter of God, and an official member of the Church.

Messiah: From the Hebrew word that means "anointed one." The Messiah was prophesied to be the one who would deliver the Jewish people from oppression.

morality: The principles that determine whether something is right or wrong, good or evil.

CLOSING PRAYER

"Lord our God, we commit ourselves to serving you as our King. We also commit to serving those around us as we share in your reign. May we open our hearts to others instead of remaining distant. Help us to seek you in all that we do. In Jesus' name, we pray. Amen."

Lesson Six
Exile – Return – Maccabean Revolt

| Exile | 2 Kings 17–25 |

| Return | Ezra, Nehemiah |

| Maccabean Revolt | 1 Maccabees |

80 | ENCOUNTER

The Big Picture

God's light shines even in the darkest moments. This lesson is about a dark time in Israel's history. God's Chosen People had become a kingdom—the kingdom of Israel—but the kingdom had split. Foreign powers conquered them, and the Israelites now faced exile and the destruction of Solomon's Temple.

Still, God's light shone through those who were faithful. The prophet Daniel is a great example. He was faithful to God even in the most extreme circumstances— even when he was face to face with lions.

OPENING PRAYER

"Lord God, you are faithful to us always. In tough times, you are close. Help our hearts to know and trust you every day, in every situation. Give us the grace to be faithful and have confidence in you. May we learn from the faithful men and women of Scripture and imitate their trust in you. In Jesus' name, we pray. Amen."

REMEMBER THIS!

> "When you pass through the waters I will be with you; and through the rivers, they shall not overwhelm you; when you walk through fire you shall not be burned, and the flame shall not consume you."
>
> —Isaiah 43:2

God is faithful. The Bible shows us in this lesson how true that is—in tough times, exile, and even a lion's den. Through the prophet Isaiah, God speaks to us about his faithfulness. He doesn't promise that things will be easy, fun, or comfortable. But God does promise that he will be with us and that he will bring us through whatever happens.

What a powerful promise! Keep this verse close to your heart for tough times. Hard math test? Your team is losing by fifty points? Someone has hurt your heart? In all these situations, remember: "The flame shall not consume you!"

WARM UP

Prophets

Dorothy Day was a writer and social activist who might be a canonized saint one day. She wrote to "comfort the afflicted and afflict the comfortable."* That is what **PROPHETS** do. They give us hope when things are tough but also challenge us to keep growing.

In these hypothetical scenarios, how could you be someone who both comforts and challenges others?

Your friend reads at a school Mass but stumbles and struggles through the reading. Some other kids laugh at her mistakes, and she is really embarrassed. You see her after Mass, and she looks upset. _____

_____

_____

Your brother has started to spend more time with a new group of friends. You notice that his habits are changing for the worse. He is cursing, talking about inappropriate things, and being mean to his old friends. _____

_____

_____

Your mom has had a really awful day. You get home from school and can immediately sense it. She doesn't talk about it, but you can tell that she's having a tough time.

_____

_____

_____

You notice some kids making fun of your friend because he goes to the parish youth group. You are upset but also afraid they will make fun of you, too. Something tells you that you should speak up. _____

_____

_____

*James Allaire and Rosemary Broughton, introduction to *Praying with Dorothy Day* (Frederick, MD: Word Among Us Press, 1995).

Lesson Six – Exile – Return – Maccabean Revolt | 83

TIME PERIOD OVERVIEW

Exile, Return, and Maccabean Revolt

On your *Bible Timeline* chart, look for the Exile (baby blue), Return (yellow), and Maccabean Revolt (orange) panels. You'll find the stories of this period in 2 Kings, Ezra, Nehemiah, and 1 Maccabees.

In our last lesson, we saw that most of Israel's kings were disasters. They were unfaithful to God, and some even worshiped the idols of false gods. Even the better kings, like Solomon and David, committed serious sins. The kings' selfishness and sin always brought trouble to the people.

After Solomon came his son Rehoboam, who greedily taxed the people and caused great suffering. The people rebelled, and Israel split into two weak kingdoms. The northern kingdom was conquered by the Assyrians and eventually disappeared. The southern kingdom of Judah lasted a little longer but was conquered by the Babylonians, who took the people captive and made them slaves.

84 | ENCOUNTER

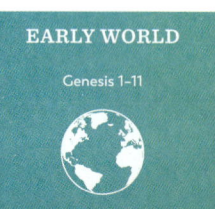

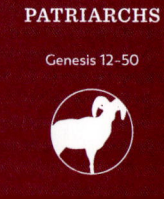

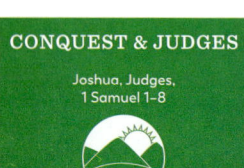

EARLY WORLD	PATRIARCHS	EGYPT & EXODUS	DESERT WANDERINGS	CONQUEST & JUDGES	ROYAL KINGDOM
Genesis 1–11	Genesis 12–50	Exodus	Numbers	Joshua, Judges, 1 Samuel 1–8	1 Samuel 9–31, 2 Samuel, 1 Kings 1–11

HANUKKAH

After the Maccabeans defeated the Greeks, they returned to Jerusalem to find the Temple in ruins. The people went to work immediately. They repaired the Temple, purified it, and made new holy vessels. Finally, they rededicated the Temple to God, celebrating with songs and thanksgiving for eight days (2 Maccabees 10:1–8).

Jewish tradition tells us that a miracle occurred at the rededication, for the people could find only a small jar of oil to burn in the Temple menorah—enough oil for one day. But the oil lasted miraculously through all eight days!

If you have Jewish friends, you know that Jews still celebrate the rededication of the Temple and the miracle of the oil every year during the eight days of Hanukkah.

But God's light shone in the darkness of the **EXILE**, especially in the lives of people like Daniel, who remained loyal to God even when it meant risking his life.

After the Exile, the people returned from Babylon in stages. They were now called Jews because their homeland was Judah. Their beautiful Temple had been destroyed, and Jerusalem lay in ruins—so they got to work. They rebuilt the Temple, renewed the covenant, and rebuilt Jerusalem's walls.

Even though they were still ruled by different conquering empires, the Jews lived in relative peace for many years. But when they were living under Greek rule, they could not worship God freely, and the people rebelled. Judas Maccabeus and his brothers led an uprising that Jews still celebrate now, every Hanukkah.

If You Ask Me

- Have you ever felt betrayed by someone who was supposed to be a friend? What was the experience like? How hard was it for you to forgive them?
- Why do you think God remained faithful to the Israelites even though they repeatedly failed to stay faithful to him?

DIVIDED KINGDOM	EXILE	RETURN	MACCABEAN REVOLT	MESSIANIC FULFILLMENT	THE CHURCH
1 Kings 12–22 2 Kings 1–16	2 Kings 17–25	Ezra Nehemiah	1 Maccabees	Luke	Acts

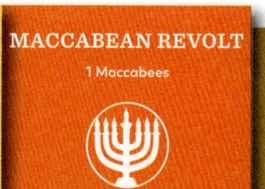

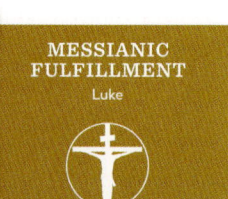

Dive In Video

Exile, Return, Maccabean Revolt . . . .**Mark Hart**

"Sometimes the light of God is clearest in the darkest moments." —Mark H.

During the video, Mark will ask you to pause and read two Bible stories. Find and mark them in your Bibles now so that you can open to them quickly when you need to:
- *Daniel 6:16–23, Daniel in the Lion's Den*
- *Ezra 3:10–11, Worship Restored in Jerusalem*

DIVE IN

In the dark period of exile, Daniel stands out as a light. Daniel was one of the Jews enslaved in Babylon. He was a holy and prayerful man; though he was a captive, he even impressed the Babylonian king, Nebuchadnezzar. Like Joseph in Genesis, Daniel became an important advisor to Nebuchadnezzar and the kings who came after him.

Other advisors became jealous of Daniel's special favor and hatched a plan to destroy him. They convinced the king that he was a god, so anyone who prayed to another god must be a threat. The king agreed and issued new laws that made praying to another god punishable by death. Meanwhile, Daniel remained faithful and prayed to God as he always had—so Daniel's enemies pounced, accusing him of breaking the king's new laws.

The king faced a dilemma. He had to enforce his own laws so he would not appear weak, but he also really liked Daniel and did not wish to kill him. But his pride won. The king sent Daniel to certain death in the lion's den, telling him, "May your God, whom you serve continually, deliver you" (Daniel 6:16). To everyone's astonishment, God did just that! The hungry lions refused to touch Daniel, and he survived miraculously.

Daniel's story shows God's faithfulness even in dark, terrible times. The Israelites were once again enslaved. They had been unfaithful to God, but God remained faithful to them. Eventually, God worked through Cyrus, the king of Persia, to bring them out of slavery in Babylon.

When Jews returned to the Promised Land, their hearts were still far from the Lord. In Babylon, they had adopted many false gods, just as they had when they were slaves in Egypt. Now, again, they needed God to cleanse their hearts. They had forgotten God's law, the Temple had been destroyed, and they had fallen into idolatry.

But God continued to be faithful. Upon their return, God sent prophets and great leaders like Haggai, Ezra, and Nehemiah. Haggai and Nehemiah led them to rebuild the Temple and the city of Jerusalem. Ezra encouraged them, teaching them about God's law and leading them to renew the covenant with God.

> "Do not be grieved, for the joy of the Lord is your strength."
>
> —Nehemiah 8:10

If You Ask Me

- Is there anyone in your life or in our world today who reminds you of Daniel because of his or her faithfulness, even during difficulty? How does this person show faithfulness?
- Who are some "prophets" that God sends to our modern society to remind us of our faith?

Got It?

1. The story of the prophet Daniel is similar in some ways to the story of _____ in the book of Genesis.

    a. Adam

    b. Joseph

    c. Abraham

    d. Noah

2. God miraculously saved Daniel from execution by _____.

    a. lions

    b. a firing squad

    c. drowning

    d. burning

3. Which of these was the pagan king God used to send the Jews home from exile?

    a. Daniel

    b. Cyrus

    c. Ezra

    d. Nehemiah

DIVE IN ACTIVITY

Prophets of Hope

Sometimes people have to leave their homes and live as strangers somewhere else, as the Israelites did in Babylon. It is hard to live away from your home.

Some people who once had a home in your community are struggling to live somewhere else now. They might be in hospitals, nursing homes, or deployed on military service. They might be in homeless shelters or prisons. Some people may be living in your community as strangers because they had to flee a war or persecution in their homeland.

Remember that you are a prophet, too! We can each be a prophetic voice in our community and speak God's hope to others. Write a letter or card to share God's encouragement with a person "in exile." (Your teacher or leader may give you a specific assignment.) Exercise your calling to bring God's hope to those who need it most.

BIBLICAL CHARACTER VIDEO

Esther . . . . Chika Anyanwu

"'O God, whose might is over all, hear the voice of the despairing, and save us from the hands of evildoers. And save me from my fear!'" —Esther 14:19

BIBLICAL CHARACTER PROFILE

Esther

Chika says she is a good runner. But she isn't talking about racing or marathons—she's talking about running away from tough or awkward situations. She used to distract herself, run away from apologizing, and avoid situations that made her uncomfortable. But as she grew, she learned to live out the words of St. Paul to St. Timothy: God has given us a spirit of "power and love and self-control" (2 Timothy 1:7).

Chika found herself in an extremely uncomfortable situation after a dinner where someone had used racist stereotypes. Chika realized that nobody else was going to say anything. Despite her urge to run and avoid it, she made a different choice. She decided to speak to the man who had made the comments. Chika asked her friends to pray for her to have wisdom, charity, and fortitude. She fasted. Finally, she was ready to have a conversation with him. He was surprisingly receptive and repented for what he had said.

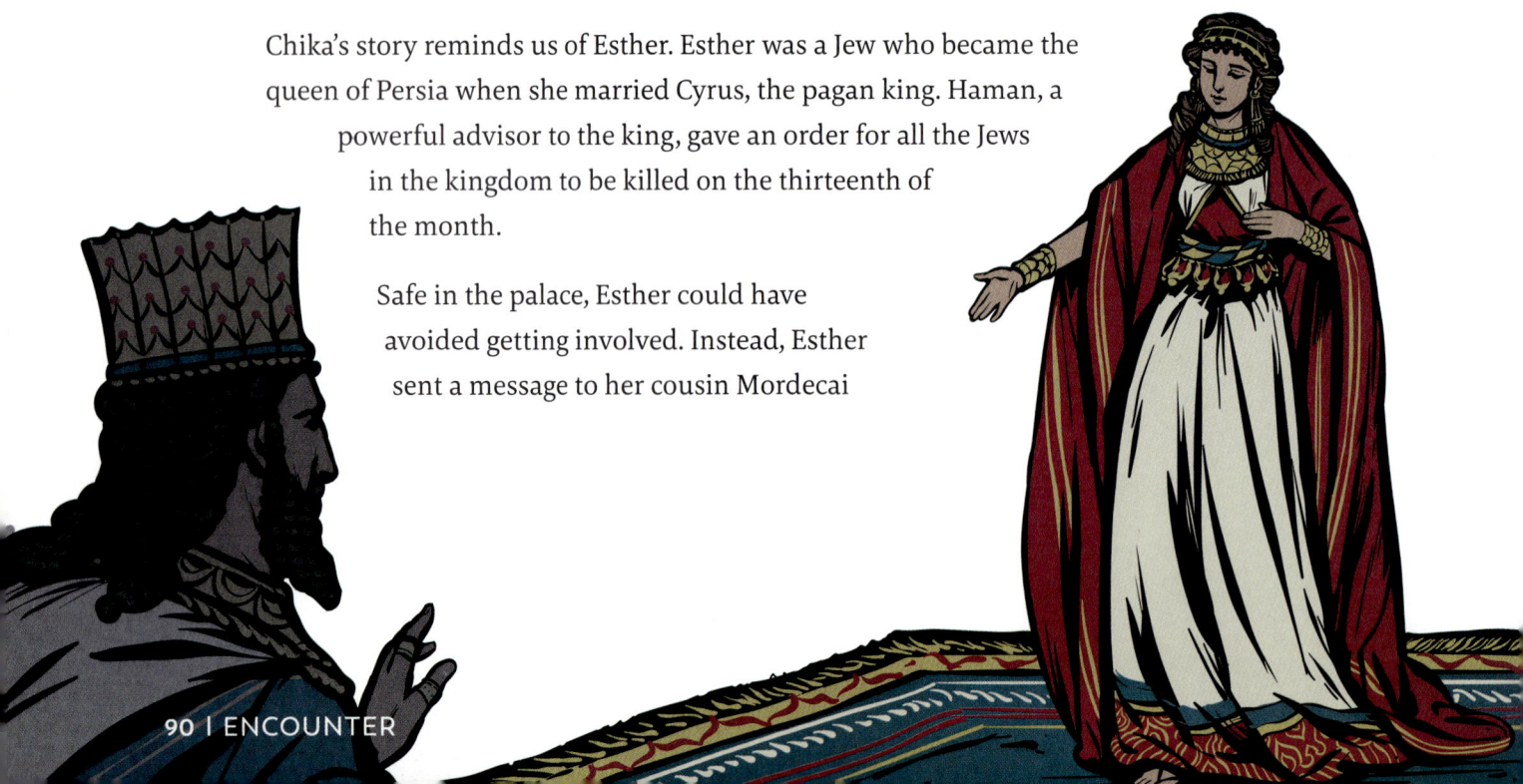

Chika's story reminds us of Esther. Esther was a Jew who became the queen of Persia when she married Cyrus, the pagan king. Haman, a powerful advisor to the king, gave an order for all the Jews in the kingdom to be killed on the thirteenth of the month.

Safe in the palace, Esther could have avoided getting involved. Instead, Esther sent a message to her cousin Mordecai

90 | ENCOUNTER

to gather all the Jews for a three-day fast. She too fasted and prayed. On the third day, Esther did something extremely dangerous: she approached King Cyrus without an invitation. (This was not allowed and could have cost her life.) But Esther was strengthened by the prayers and the fasting of her community. She didn't run but went forward courageously, empowered by prayer. She asked the king to spare the Jews, and he did. She spoke up for her people and saved them.

Chika's and Esther's stories remind us that prayer and fasting—both our own and that of others—can give us great courage.

Fast and Pray

Find Esther on your *Bible Timeline* chart. What period is her story in? Now read Esther's prayer in **Esther 14:1–19**.

Think about opportunities to fast and pray in your own life. Fasting can help us build strength and discipline. It is also a way for us to pray. Fasting, even in small ways, helps focus our hearts on hearing God more clearly. Think about the concrete ways you can offer more fasting and prayer.

I can fast from food and also from _____

_____.

Like Esther, I can fast and pray when I witness injustice and want to stand up for what is right; I can also fast and pray when/for _____

_____.

Assyria Conquers the Northern Kingdom . . . . 2 Kings 17:6–8
Babylon Conquers Jerusalem . . . . 2 Kings 24:10–17
Zerubbabel Rebuilds the Temple . . . . Ezra 5:2
Ezra Reads the Book of the Law . . . . Nehemiah 8:1–3, 9–10
Judas Maccabeus Leads the Revolt . . . . 1 Maccabees 3:1–9
The Maccabees Purify the Temple. . . . . 1 Maccabees 4:36–58

Find Out More

Exile, Return, and Maccabean Revolt

Here are more stories you can read from the times of Exile and Return, along with two stories about Judas Maccabeus and his brothers.

Living It Out

This lesson has addressed some dark times. How can we live out what we have learned through the stories of God's faithful prophets?

- Be consistent in prayer like Daniel. Keep talking to God no matter how well or how badly things are going. Prayer is not only for times we feel close to God but for *all* times. God wants to hear from you no matter what you are experiencing. Even in the toughest times, God will not leave you alone or abandon you.

- Be patient. God's deliverance and plan often follow a different timeline than what we want. Sometimes we go through hard things and wonder if God is still with us. Yes, he is! Always! A tough time is never a sign that God has abandoned us, but it may be a time for us to grow in trust when we aren't sure how things will work out.

- Be prophetic. God wants to speak through you. Listen for God's voice. Listen as he comforts and challenges you to do better and change accordingly. Ask God to show you when to offer others comfort or a challenge.

92 | ENCOUNTER

WORDPLAY

exile: To be forced from your native home and have to live somewhere else. During the Exile period, God's people were conquered by their enemies and led away from the Promised Land.

prophets: Individuals chosen by God to proclaim God's will to the people and call everyone to live according to the covenant.

CLOSING PRAYER

"Lord God, we can imagine what it was like for the Israelites who lived in exile. The world around us tempts us too to turn away from you, and sometimes we struggle. Give us the courage to be faithful to you, just as Daniel and Esther were. Help us to trust you everywhere we go and in everything we do. When we are afraid, teach us to fast and pray so that we may grow strong in you. In Jesus' name, we pray. Amen."

Lesson Seven

Messianic Fulfillment: Jesus and the Gospels

MESSIANIC FULFILLMENT LUKE

The Big Picture

The center of history. The world's most important event. The greatest thing that ever happened: God became one of us.

God the Son became man and was born in Bethlehem. He is the Messiah, the Savior whom the prophets foretold. Jesus is the one who restores our friendship with God. In his life and ministry, Jesus made clear everything about who God is and who we are. Then by his **Passion**, death, and Resurrection, he proved to be the ultimate hero who won the greatest victory—saving not just the moment or the day, but life itself. Jesus suffered, died, and rose from the dead so that you and I could have eternal life.

OPENING PRAYER

"Lord Jesus, you are the Word made flesh. You are the ultimate hero who came to set me free. Today I am yours. I am sorry for my sins, and I offer you my heart. You are the Savior of the world and my Savior. Open my mind to learn more about your love today. In your name, we pray. Amen."

Lesson Seven – Messianic Fulfillment: Jesus and the Gospels

REMEMBER THIS!

> "For God so loved the world that he gave his only-begotten Son, that whoever believes in him should not perish but have eternal life."
>
> —John 3:16

Jesus spoke these words to a Jewish rabbi named Nicodemus. Nicodemus was interested in Jesus and his work, but he was nervous about what others would think of his curiosity—so he met with Jesus in secret. He had many questions for Jesus. In his answers, Jesus shared the heart of his mission. (You can read the story of Nicodemus' secret meeting with Jesus in John 3:1–21.)

The reason Jesus came into the world is summed up in this verse. Jesus is the perfect image of the Father's love, sent for our salvation. Keep this verse in your heart and hold on to this important truth. Use the verse as a prayer, and don't be afraid to share it and proclaim it to others.

WARM UP

Who Is Jesus?

Who is Jesus? What did he come to do? This lesson will dive into the heart of Jesus' life and ministry. To get started, reflect on who Jesus is. How do you picture his face? What do you think his favorite food was? Did he have any special hobbies? Where did he like to spend time by himself?

Draw a picture of Jesus as you imagine him. Along with your drawing, list several things you'd like to know about Jesus. You can choose small things, like his favorite color, or deeper things, like his personal fears. Or list several things you think everyone should know about him.

Things I would like to know about Jesus: _____

_____

_____

Things everyone should know about Jesus: _____

_____

_____

Lesson Seven – Messianic Fulfillment: Jesus and the Gospels

TIME PERIOD OVERVIEW

Messianic Fulfillment

On your *Bible Timeline* chart, look for the **Messianic Fulfillment** panel (gold). This is the period of Jesus' life on earth, the heart of history. It is when all the Old Testament covenants, all God's promises, and all humanity's hopes are fulfilled. We will follow the story in the **GOSPEL** of Luke, and it is also found in the Gospels of Matthew, Mark, and John.

The Old Testament gave us a glimpse of God's ultimate plan. Every single thing so far has led to the ultimate hero of that plan: Jesus.

No matter how much his Chosen People messed up, God never stopped loving them and never abandoned his covenant. Nor will God ever stop loving us. What he wants most from each of us is our heart. He proved this once and for all in Jesus. God didn't send another prophet, priest, or king to deliver his people. He sent his only Son—the highest prophet, priest, and king of all.

When he arrived on earth, God's Son didn't descend from the clouds. He didn't ride in with an army of angels. He quietly slipped into the world like any other child. This is called **THE INCARNATION**—

98 | ENCOUNTER

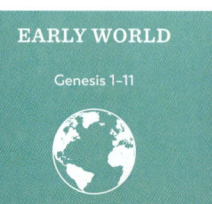

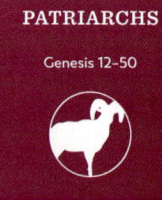

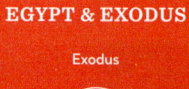

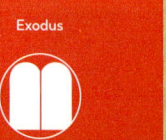

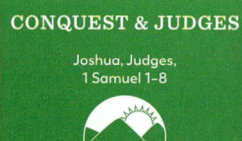

EARLY WORLD	PATRIARCHS	EGYPT & EXODUS	DESERT WANDERINGS	CONQUEST & JUDGES	ROYAL KINGDOM
Genesis 1–11	Genesis 12–50	Exodus	Numbers	Joshua, Judges, 1 Samuel 1–8	1 Samuel 9–31, 2 Samuel, 1 Kings 1–11

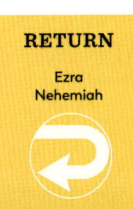

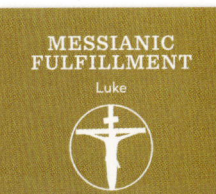

when God took on a human body and became one of us. Conceived by the Holy Spirit, born of the Virgin Mary, Jesus was known for most of his life only by his family and close neighbors. As he grew up, it's possible that nobody saw him as anyone special. He spent most of his life working as a carpenter, quietly praying and turning his heart to the Father as he waited for his public ministry to begin.

When that time came, Jesus was baptized in the Jordan River by John the Baptist, and then he went into the desert to pray and fast for forty days. Satan tried to tempt him there with promises of worldly power, but Jesus resisted him (Luke 4:1–15).

Jesus relied wholly on God, often going off by himself to be with the Father and pray. The *Catechism* tells us that his prayer was "humble and trusting" (CCC 2600). Jesus prayed at his baptism (Luke 3:21–22), and he prayed all night before choosing his twelve Apostles (Luke 6:12–13). Jesus was praying when Peter confessed that he was the Christ (which is the Greek word for the Messiah, the "anointed one"), and he was praying as he was **TRANSFIGURED**, appearing in all his glory in front of Peter, James, and John (Luke 9:18–20, 29). Jesus was also praying when one of his followers asked him to teach them to pray; that's when Jesus taught them the **OUR FATHER** (Luke 11:1–4).

Jesus also taught his followers to pray for their enemies (Luke 6:28), to persevere in prayer (Luke 11:5–13), and to pray simply and humbly (Luke 18:9–14).

On the night before he died, Jesus prayed so earnestly in the Garden of Gethsemane that he sweated blood (Luke 22:39–46). The following day, his final words on the **CROSS** were to the Father: "Into your hands I commit my spirit!" (Luke 23:46).

Jesus is our **REDEEMER**, our Savior, and our Lord. Being made perfect through prayer, suffering, and obedience, he became "the source of eternal salvation to all who obey him" (Hebrews 5:9).

If You Ask Me

- What stories from the Old Testament remind you of Jesus' life?
- Why do we (and the Israelites) need a divine Savior? Why weren't the prophets, priests, and kings of the Old Testament enough?
- What do prophets, priests, and kings do? How can you participate in Jesus' mission as a prophet? A priest? A king?

Messianic Fulfillment ....Mark Hart

DIVE IN VIDEO

"The paralyzed guy couldn't help himself. The four friends understood that Jesus could *help him. We need friends like that. We need to* be *friends like that."* —Mark H.

During the video, Mark will ask you to pause and read three Bible stories. Find and mark them in your Bibles now so that you can open to them quickly when you need to:
- *Luke 4:1–13, The Temptation of Jesus*
- *Luke 5:17–26, The Paralyzed Man and His Friends*
- *Luke 24:13–31, The Walk to Emmaus*

DIVE IN

In a desert outside Jerusalem, Satan watched as Jesus prayed and fasted. Satan didn't yet know exactly who Jesus was. Son of God? What did that mean? Satan did know one thing: Jesus was different. This time, God wasn't coming after Pharaoh, the Amalekites, Goliath, or the Babylonians. This time, death itself was the target. Satan knew that something had to be done to stop this Jesus.

Satan got to work, using his standard strategy of fear and lies. As Jesus fasted and prayed in the desert, Satan whispered, "If you're really the Son of God…" and tempted Jesus with a series of dares (Luke 4:3–11). But he couldn't trick Jesus, not even when Jesus was tired, hungry, and alone. True God and true man, Jesus was like us in all things, including temptation—but never sin.

Jesus challenged everything that humanity expected and everything that was possible. He preached with authority, forgave sins, and gave us the Beatitudes, blessing the poor and those who mourn. He calmed a storm with his words, multiplied loaves and fish, walked on water, healed the deaf and the blind, cured **LEPERS**, cast out demons, and raised the dead—all in front of many witnesses. Even people who didn't care much for faith or religion wanted to see this carpenter from Galilee perform miracles. Meanwhile, Jesus' mission made the religious leaders suspicious. They saw Jesus as a threat. Yet massive crowds of the poor and needy kept coming to see him. Jesus offered them something more than physical healing, something nobody else had ever offered before.

You can find an example of this in Luke 5:17–26. The friends of a paralyzed man had heard of Jesus and were determined to bring their friend before him. But the house where Jesus was teaching was too crowded to enter, so they took off part of the roof and lowered their paralyzed friend down to Jesus from there. What determined and faithful friends! Jesus did indeed heal the man's body—but more importantly, he satisfied the needs of his heart and soul.

The Paralyzed Man

"Finding no way to bring him in, because of the crowd, they went up on the roof and let him down with his bed through the tiles into their midst before Jesus. And when he saw their faith he said, 'Man, your sins are forgiven you. ... Rise, take up your bed and go home.'"

—Luke 5:19-20, 24

Jesus grew in fame but not necessarily in popularity. People from all over Judea wanted to see his amazing works, but Jesus also had difficult teachings that some people resisted. For example, Jesus said that his flesh would be real food and his blood would be real drink (John 6:55). Even his own disciples didn't fully understand what this meant.

Three years into his ministry, as he celebrated the Passover meal with his friends, Jesus knew what suffering awaited him. That night he took bread in his hands and gave it to them, saying, "This is my body which is given for you" (Luke 22:19). Then he took a cup of wine and gave it to them, saying, "This chalice which is poured out for you is the new covenant in my blood" (Luke 22:20). This event is called the **LAST SUPPER**. It was Jesus' last meal with his friends and the first Eucharist, the sign of the **NEW AND EVERLASTING COVENANT**.

The Last Supper by Juan de Juanes

Up to this point, the people had offered ritual sacrifices in the Temple. But in Jesus, God himself became the sacrifice—the final one. Only Jesus, true God and true Man, could offer the perfect and unrepeatable sacrifice for all time and for all people in his **PASSION** and death. The Temple sacrifices were no longer needed.

Jesus had predicted his own death several times, which made everyone uncomfortable. The jealous leaders had continued to plot against him, trying to find an opportunity to execute him—and they finally found it during Passover. Judas, one of Jesus' closest followers, betrayed him that night. Judas led the authorities to Jesus, they arrested him on false charges, and his friends deserted him in fear. Jesus was accused, abandoned, beaten, mocked, and finally condemned to death.

When Jesus was nailed to the Cross and died, his enemies thought they had won. But how wrong they were! God had been planning this offering all along. From the moment of the Fall, God had been gathering his people so that they could know him and serve him in holiness. He had chosen the Israelites and called them to himself through the covenants, teaching them and preparing their hearts for the Savior.

But, over and over again, people turned away from God, breaking their promises and committing horrible sins. They deserved the punishment and desperately needed a Savior.

We are the same.

Jesus took our punishment and died in agony. Why? Because he loves us. And he won't ever stop loving us. Jesus offered the perfect sacrifice—himself—which broke the power of sin and death forever. And he rose again so that we could, too.

Jesus isn't just a teacher or a healer or someone who says wise things. He is Emmanuel, "God with us." He's the Savior—*your* Savior. Only Jesus and no one else conquered death so that your sins could be forgiven and you could live with him forever in heaven.

If You Ask Me

- How would you answer the question, "Who is Jesus?"
- How would you answer the question, "What did Jesus come to do?"
- What stories about Jesus do you like most? Why are these stories meaningful to you?

THE EVENT THAT CHANGED THE WORLD

Jesus rose from the dead. We call this extraordinary event the Resurrection.

Jesus truly died on the Cross. The Gospel of John tells us that to make sure he was dead, a soldier used his spear to pierce Jesus' side, and blood and water poured from the wound. Jesus' "death was a real death, ... [the] end of his earthly human existence" (CCC 627).

His followers anointed his body with spices and wrapped it in linen cloths, as was the Jewish custom back then. Then they laid his body in a cave-like tomb sealed with a huge stone.

Early in the morning on the third day following his crucifixion, Mary Magdalene and other holy women came to the tomb to finish anointing his body. What they saw frightened them: the stone at the entrance had been rolled away. Inside, the linen cloths were lying where Jesus' body had been—but his body was gone. The tomb was empty!

What had happened? Had someone stolen the body? Soon the women understood. The Risen Christ appeared to them and spoke to them. Then he appeared to Peter and the other Apostles. Jesus had risen from the dead! Over the next forty days, Jesus spoke with the Apostles many times and even ate with them. On one occasion, he appeared to more than five hundred people.

Jesus' glorified body was different from our earthly bodies. We aren't sure exactly what it was like, but we know from Scripture that some people didn't recognize him at first, though they knew him when he spoke to them or broke bread with them. We know that his skin showed the wounds of his crucifixion. We also know that he could appear and disappear without warning, yet he was not a ghost. He ate with the Apostles, spoke to them, and walked with them.

The Resurrection changed human history. By it, Jesus opened a path to new life, eternal life, for us. The Resurrection is proof that Jesus is God's Son, the confirmation of his teachings and miracles, and the promise of our future resurrection.

Christ's Appearance to Mary Magdalene after the Resurrection by Alexander Ivanov

Lesson Seven – Messianic Fulfillment: Jesus and the Gospels | 103

Got It

1. Jesus successfully resisted the devil's attacks when Jesus was _____.

    a. healing people in the Temple

    b. sleeping and dreaming

    c. eating a meal with his friends

    d. praying and fasting in the desert

2. In the video, Mark focused on the healing of a _____ man whose friends helped him get to Jesus.

    a. blind

    b. deaf

    c. paralyzed

    d. left-handed

3. Jesus is _____.

    a. the Savior

    b. a Gentile

    c. a prince

    d. a wise guru

DIVE IN ACTIVITY

Visio Divina

Here are three pictures of Jesus painted by different artists at different times in the Church's history. Pick one of these images that speaks to you. Describe what you notice about Jesus in this image.

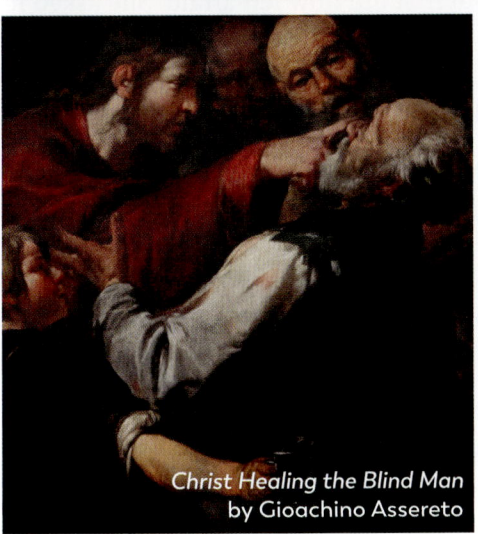

Jesus and the Samaritan Woman by Veronese

Christ Healing the Blind Man by Gioachino Assereto

Ascension of Christ by Garofalo

_____

_____

_____

_____

Lesson Seven – Messianic Fulfillment: Jesus and the Gospels | 105

BIBLICAL CHARACTER VIDEO

The Boy with the Loaves and Fish . . . . Ashley Hinojosa

"Andrew, Simon Peter's brother, said to [Jesus],
'There is a lad here who has five barley loaves and two fish;
but what are they among so many?'" —John 6:8–9

BIBLICAL CHARACTER PROFILE

The Boy with the Loaves and Fish

Ashley shared her story about being called to study theology. She knew there would be challenges. She would have to move, make new friends, adapt, and somehow come up with money for tuition. She had no idea how she would do it, but she still felt called by God to go.

Deciding to follow God's call brought her joy and peace at first, but later she had many questions and fears. One day at Mass, she prayed about everything. She told God that she had been confident at first but now felt afraid. She asked for his strength.

After Mass, she returned a missed call as she walked to her car. She had been chosen for a big scholarship that would cover all her tuition! This was an amazing sign for her about how God will provide what we need when we need it.

This story reminds us of the multiplication of loaves in John 6. More than five thousand hungry people had gathered to hear Jesus. A boy offered to share his five loaves and two fish, even though that was nowhere near enough food to feed the huge crowd. But Jesus took the boy's offering and miraculously multiplied it—so much so that after everyone ate, there were twelve baskets of leftovers! The boy had been willing to give even what little he had, and God used it to feed thousands.

We can have faith that Jesus always sees us and never leaves us wanting. Like the boy with the loaves and fish, Ashley trusted God and stepped out in faith; God did the rest. What may seem impossible to us is not impossible for God.

106 | ENCOUNTER

My Loaves and Fish

Find "The Miracles of Jesus" on your *Bible Timeline* chart. Now read the story of the loaves and fish in **John 6:3–13**.

You have something to offer. Don't ever doubt this or compare yourself to others. God has given you something special to share with others. If you let him, he can and will multiply it.

Complete the following exercise to identify what you can offer to Jesus.

- What are some things people say you're good at?
- What are some things you like doing?
- What are some ways you like to help others?
- What is a need that you see in your community?
- Who do you feel called to serve?

Find Out More

Major Events of Jesus' Life

An Angel Announces Jesus' Birth to Mary	LUKE 1:26–38
Jesus Is Born in Bethlehem	LUKE 2:1–7
Jesus Is Baptized	LUKE 3:21–22
Jesus Fasts and Is Tempted in the Desert	LUKE 4:1–13
Jesus Changes Water to Wine at a Wedding	JOHN 2:1–12
Jesus Preaches the Sermon on the Mount	LUKE 6:17–49
Jesus Gives Peter the Keys to the Kingdom	MATTHEW 16:13–20
Jesus Is Transfigured in Glory	LUKE 9:28–36
Jesus Institutes the Eucharist	LUKE 22:14–20
Jesus Is Crucified	LUKE 23:32–49
Jesus Rises from the Dead	LUKE 24:1–12
Jesus Ascends into Heaven	LUKE 24:49–53

Jesus is the Son of God, the Word made flesh. Everything he said and did when he lived on earth shows us who God is.

A good way to learn more about Jesus is to read the Gospels: Matthew, Mark, Luke, and John. A good Gospel to start with is the Gospel of Luke.

Living It Out

How should a follower of Jesus live? Think of someone you know whom you would consider a present-day follower of Jesus. It might be someone in your parish or even someone in your family. Talk to that person this week about following Jesus. What would you like to ask him or her about Jesus? Here are some questions to get you started:

- How did he or she come to know Jesus?
- What is the most important thing he or she does every day to stay close to him?

108 | ENCOUNTER

WORDPLAY

Cross: In the Roman Empire, crucifixion was a form of execution carried out by nailing or binding a person to a wooden cross. Jesus' Cross has since become a universal Christian symbol of Christ's sacrifice and victory over sin and death.

Gospel: From the Old English words meaning "good news." In the New Testament, the four Gospels detail the life, teachings, miracles, death, and Resurrection of Jesus.

Incarnation, the: From the word "incarnate," which means to take on flesh or human form. Through the Incarnation, God the Son assumed a human body, was born of Mary, and became man.

Last Supper: The Passover meal that Jesus ate with his Apostles on the same night as his betrayal and arrest. It was during this meal that he instituted the Eucharist.

lepers: People who contracted the disease of leprosy. According to the Law of Moses, lepers were unclean and had to live away from other people.

New and Everlasting Covenant: The final, perpetual covenant that God made with the entire human family through Jesus, making it possible for us to dwell with him in heaven for eternity.

Our Father: Also called the "Lord's Prayer." This prayer that Jesus taught his disciples is considered a summary of the whole Gospel.

Passion, the: The time of Jesus' suffering, from his agony in the Garden of Gethsemane through his arrest, trial, and crucifixion.

Redeemer, Redemption: From a Latin word meaning "to buy back." Jesus is our Redeemer because he paid the price for us with his own blood and saved us from sin and death.

transfigured: Transformed into something better or more beautiful.

CLOSING PRAYER

"Lord Jesus, you gave everything to your Father. You loved perfectly and triumphantly. Help me now to do the same. I claim you as my Lord and Savior. I reject and repent of my sins. I am yours, Jesus. In your name, we pray. Amen."

Lesson Eight
The Church (and Your Role in It)

THE CHURCH ACTS

The Big Picture

This lesson covers the early Church, but it isn't just a history lesson: it is about how Christians live. The New Testament shows us how the first Christians learned to live out the Faith in their own time and spread the word about Jesus. They were entrusted with sharing the Good News (Gospel)—and they shared it far and wide. They shared the Gospel even when they knew they could be killed because of it, just as Jesus was.

With the help of the Holy Spirit, we are called to do the same. The words of St. Luke, St. Paul, and other sacred authors are real and relevant to you **today**. The lessons of the early Church can apply to the adventure of your life at school, on your team, in your family, at your parish, and even in your personal prayer life.

OPENING PRAYER

"God the Holy Spirit, you came upon the disciples at Pentecost and empowered the early Church in its mission. Come upon us again today. Capture our minds, hearts, and imaginations with the same mission to share the Good News with the world. Help us continue the mission of Jesus wherever we are. Inspire us and empower us. In Jesus' name, we pray. Amen."

REMEMBER THIS!

> "And behold, I send the promise of my Father upon you; but stay in the city, until you are clothed with power from on high."
>
> —Luke 24:49

Jesus promised his closest followers, the Apostles, that when he returned to the Father, he would send them an **ADVOCATE**: the Holy Spirit. This promise was fulfilled at Pentecost when the Apostles were filled with the Spirit and were able to courageously proclaim the Gospel.

Through your Baptism and Confirmation, the same Holy Spirit is poured out and unleashed in your soul.

The Father's promise is for the Church both in the time of the Apostles and now! When the Holy Spirit moves in your heart, don't be afraid to be a witness for Jesus wherever you are.

WARM UP

Empowered!

The story of the early Church isn't just about historical events; it's a reminder of God's power, both then and now. Let's ask God to empower us. We can be confident that the same Holy Spirit who empowered the Apostles is alive and active in the Church today.

Unscramble these words to learn what gifts the Holy Spirit gave to the Apostles (find clues at CCC 1831). God desires to pour out these same gifts on us so we can thrive in our identity and mission.

egdolwnke _____

olusnec _____

dmosiw _____

tiepy _____

refa fo het dolr _____

edforutit _____

usatdnidregnn _____

Lesson Eight – The Church (and Your Role in It) | 113

TIME PERIOD OVERVIEW

The Church

Pentecost by Jean Restout

What a journey we have taken! Now we have arrived at the final lesson. The first six lessons told the story of God's Chosen People, the Israelites. The seventh lesson covered the coming of God's Son, Jesus, and the mystery of his life, his death, and the Resurrection. This final lesson describes the early Church as Christians began to live out the New Covenant. This history is told mostly in the Acts of the Apostles, which was written by St. Luke. Acts picks up where the Gospel of Luke ends. On your *Bible Timeline* chart, look for the Church panel (white).

After the Resurrection, Jesus spent forty days with his Apostles. He commanded them to preach to all people and to build his Church. He promised that he would send the Holy Spirit to empower them. That same day, as the Apostles looked on, Jesus ascended into heaven. Trusting his promise, the Apostles prayed and waited for him to send the Holy Spirit.

EARLY WORLD	PATRIARCHS	EGYPT & EXODUS	DESERT WANDERINGS	CONQUEST & JUDGES	ROYAL KINGDOM
Genesis 1–11	Genesis 12–50	Exodus	Numbers	Joshua, Judges, 1 Samuel 1–8	1 Samuel 9–31, 2 Samuel, 1 Kings 1–11

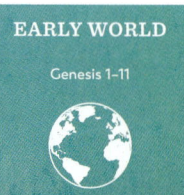

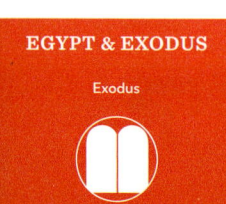

Nine days passed. (Fun fact: those nine days of prayer were the first novena!) Then, at Pentecost, the Holy Spirit came upon them like tongues of fire, and the Church was born. Suddenly the Apostles—the same ones who had run away when Jesus was arrested—became brave and joyful preachers, sharing the Gospel with everyone they met.

What did the early Church, empowered by the Holy Spirit, look like? Immediately after Pentecost, the Apostles began preaching the Gospel wherever they went. Through the power of the Holy Spirit, they healed and worked miracles, like Jesus had. Believers gathered in people's homes to read Scripture, share Jesus' message, and receive the Eucharist. The Gospel began to spread from town to town and from country to country.

As the Church formed and grew after Jesus' **ASCENSION**, miracles and wonders—along with **PERSECUTION** and even **MARTYRDOM**—were all part of the story.

> The Holy Spirit, the third Person of the Trinity, is often pictured as a dove. Other symbols for him include fire, wind, water, and anointing with oil.

If You Ask Me

- How do you imagine the Holy Spirit? How do you think the Holy Spirit could empower you in your own life?
- How do you feel about yourself as a modern disciple? How can you share the Good News where you are?
- How connected do you feel to the Church?

Lesson Eight – The Church (and Your Role in It)

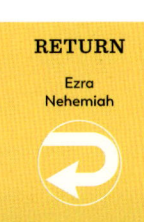

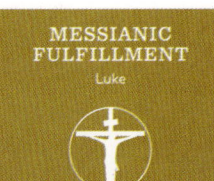

DIVIDED KINGDOM	EXILE	RETURN	MACCABEAN REVOLT	MESSIANIC FULFILLMENT	THE CHURCH
1 Kings 12–22 2 Kings 1–16	2 Kings 17–25	Ezra Nehemiah	1 Maccabees	Luke	Acts

The Church . . . . .Mark Hart

Dive In Video

"Faith is about a relationship: your relationship with Jesus." —Mark H.

During the video, Mark will ask you to pause and read three Bible stories. Find and mark them in your Bibles now so that you can open to them quickly when you need to:
- *Acts 1:21–26, The Apostles Choose Matthias to Replace Judas*
    Acts 12:1–11, Herod Imprisons Peter; Peter Escapes
- *2 Corinthians 11:23–30, Paul's Sufferings as an Apostle*

DIVE IN

The Acts of the Apostles introduces us to many people in the early Church: Priscilla and Aquila, the married evangelists; Stephen, the first deacon and martyr; Paul, the Pharisee (Jewish leader) who became an Apostle; Lydia, an early believer; and others. Life for these early Christians wasn't easy. They were resisted and mocked, and they risked their lives to follow Jesus.

> "If you continue in my word, you are truly my disciples, and you will know the truth, and the truth will make you free."
>
> —John 8:31–32

St. Paul was an unlikely Apostle, a fierce enemy of Jesus who became one of the greatest missionaries in Church history. After the Resurrection, Paul was on his way one day to arrest believers in Damascus—and Jesus appeared to him in a miraculous vision. Paul fell to the ground, blinded; Jesus told him to go to Damascus and wait. When Paul went there, the Christians in Damascus—the same ones Paul had planned to persecute—took him in, healed his blindness, and baptized him.

Paul became the Apostle to the Gentiles (non-Jews), traveling thousands of miles on missionary journeys to establish new Church communities across the Mediterranean region. As he traveled, Paul also wrote letters of advice to the new communities—letters that are preserved in the New Testament and which are read aloud at Mass.

Both St. Peter and St. Paul had dramatic adventures as they followed God's call, and both were eventually martyred (killed) for their Christian faith.

What would you do for your faith? Would you risk your life so that others could know how and why Jesus came to save them?

Our mission is the same mission that God gave to Peter and Paul: to bring others to Christ. We have the Holy Spirit to empower us and remain with us, so we know we are not alone. We have the Church to teach us and bring us the sacraments (outward signs of inner grace, instituted by God). We have the saints to pray for us. And we have our priests, our parents, and our teachers and leaders to guide us, like the people who are leading your *Encounter* program.

We stay close to Jesus through his **GRACE**, his life in our souls. Grace is his free gift to help us love him and grow in holiness. We receive grace especially through the sacraments and through prayer. Grace gives us the power to love as God loves and to know (and obey) God's will.

As you concentrate on staying close to Jesus, your mission will become clear. It will become the desire of your heart, as well as his.

Always remember who you are: an unrepeatable individual who is wanted and loved by God. He created you for greatness. He made you to be a saint.

> "I am sure that neither death, nor life, nor angels, nor principalities, nor things present, nor things to come, nor powers, nor height, nor depth, nor anything else in all creation, will be able to separate us from the love of God in Christ Jesus our Lord."
>
> —Romans 8:38–39

If You Ask Me

- What do you think it takes to be a disciple today?
- Why do you think the Holy Spirit is often depicted as a dove? As fire? As water?
- How do you feel about the idea that you were created to be a saint? What do you think that means?

Got It?

1. **Who was chosen to fill Judas' position as an Apostle?**

    a. Barnabas

    b. Aquila

    c. Matthias

    d. Ralph

2. **Many of the early Christians faced _____ for practicing their faith.**

    a. resistance

    b. mockery

    c. martyrdom

    d. all of the above

3. **Which Apostle was formerly a Pharisee and an enemy of Christianity?**

    a. Matthias

    b. Barnabas

    c. Paul

    d. Andrew

DIVE IN ACTIVITY

Letters

St. Paul wrote letters to encourage new Christian communities that were learning to live out their faith. Choose a community or person whom you would like to encourage in faith and write a letter to help inspire them. Maybe you could write to your parents or siblings, your grandparents or cousins, your classmates or teachers, or some other group. In your letter, share with them something that makes *you* want to live out your faith.

BIBLICAL CHARACTER VIDEO

Priscilla and Aquila . . . . **Chika Anyanwu**

"Greet Prisca and Aquila, my fellow workers in Christ Jesus, who risked their necks for my life, to whom not only I but also all the churches of the Gentiles give thanks." —Romans 16:3–4

BIBLICAL CHARACTER PROFILE

Priscilla and Aquila

Chika has always been told to live her life in a way that makes others ask questions. The main question she wants her life to inspire is "What is it about you?" For Chika, the answer is Jesus. Chika is still growing, but Jesus has taught her how to be kind and inviting, steadfast and charitable, courageous and forgiving, and sensitive and attentive to the needs of others.

St. Paul said he had been crucified with Christ. He no longer lived his own life; rather, Christ lived through him (Galatians 2:20). When people looked at Paul, he wanted them to see Jesus. That is exactly what happened when two tentmakers, a married couple named Priscilla and Aquila, met Paul: they saw Christ in him and became ardent followers of the Lord.

Priscilla and Aquila traveled with Paul and worked closely with him wherever they went. Once, as Priscilla and Aquila were listening to the preaching of a man named Apollos, they realized that Apollos didn't know many things about "the Way" that he needed to know. ("The Way" was what early Christianity was called.) Apollos needed more training. Instead of criticizing him for what he didn't know, Priscilla and Aquila taught him gently and encouraged him, and Apollos became a helpful and powerful preacher in the early Church.

120 | ENCOUNTER

Priscilla and Aquila made their home in whatever community they visited and even offered their own home in Rome as a church.

We are called to be like them—to live out our faith in a way that points directly to Jesus. When people meet us, our lives should make them ask, "What is it about you?" And our lives should also give the answer: "It's Jesus."

> "Now there are varieties of gifts, but the same Spirit; and there are varieties of service, but the same Lord; and there are varieties of working, but it is the same God who inspires them all in every one. To each is given the manifestation of the Spirit for the common good."
>
> —1 Corinthians 12:4–7

"There's Something Different About You"

Find the Holy Spirit on your *Bible Timeline* chart. Now read about Priscilla and Aquila in **Acts 18:1–3, 18, 24–28; Romans 16:3–4;** and **1 Corinthians 16:19**.

Chika's teaching about Priscilla and Aquila is an invitation to us. How can we live in a way that makes people ask, "What is different about you?" How can we live in a way that shows the answer is Jesus?

Priscilla and Aquila were ordinary people who were open to life in Christ. What would life in Christ look like for you? Use the prompts below to help you reflect on that.

I really enjoy _____. How can I do it in a way that glorifies God and helps others?

Sometimes I become too attached to something. (It might be a person, an activity, or a possession.) I think I'm too attached to _____. How can I let go of it to live more fully for Jesus?

Other people tell me I'm good at _____. How can I use this gift to build up his kingdom on earth?

I sometimes wish I could help other people. Who are they? What is something I could help them with? _____

What can I do every day to live for God and put him first? _____

The Apostles Receive the Gift of the Holy Spirit	Acts 2
Peter Heals a Lame Beggar	Acts 3:1–10
An Angel Frees the Apostles from Prison	Acts 5:17–21
Stephen Is Martyred	Acts 7:54–60
Paul (Saul) Is Converted on the Road to Damascus	Acts 9:1–19
Paul Escapes His Enemies in a Basket	Acts 9:23–25
Peter Escapes Prison Miraculously	Acts 12:4–11
Paul and Silas Baptize a Prison Guard and His Family	Acts 16:25–34
Priscilla and Aquila Mentor Apollos	Acts 18:24–28
Eutychus Falls from a Window as Paul Preaches	Acts 20:7–12
Paul Is Shipwrecked	Acts 27
Paul Survives a Poisonous Snake Bite	Acts 28:1–6

Find Out More

Important Events in the Acts of the Apostles

The events listed here are not necessarily the *most* important ones in the life of the early Church, but they will give you a taste of the power and joy that carried the Church forward.

Living It Out

Along this journey through Scripture, we have seen God's master plan at work. Now it's time to look for God's plan in your own life. In what ways do you see God at work? How is your story connected to the story of salvation? Your story is still being written, so there are many things in God's plan for you that have yet to unfold. But there is no doubt that he is already working in your life.

Just as we considered a timeline of salvation history and the story of God's people, consider the timeline of your life so far. What are the key events? Where has God already shown up? What blessings has God already given you? Where have you already met or felt Jesus in your life?

Consider where the timeline of your story might go next. What do you think is in the future? The closer we grow to Jesus, the more beautiful and meaningful life becomes.

Whatever else happens and wherever else your story takes you, remember that Jesus is the center. He is your best friend and companion in the epic story of your life—a story that leads all the way to heaven.

> "Having gifts that differ according to the grace given to us, let us use them: if prophecy, in proportion to our faith; if service, in our serving; he who teaches, in his teaching; he who exhorts, in his exhortation; he who contributes, in liberality; he who gives aid, with zeal; he who does acts of mercy, with cheerfulness."
>
> —Romans 12:6–8

WORDPLAY

Advocate: From a Latin word meaning "to call to one's aid"; another name for the Holy Spirit.

Ascension, the: From a Latin word meaning "to go up." The Ascension occurred forty days after the Resurrection when the Apostles witnessed Jesus go up into heaven.

grace: The divine assistance freely given to us by God, which we did not need to earn. Grace allows us to respond to God's call to become his children.

martyrdom: From a Greek word meaning "witness." A martyr gives up his or her life in defense of the Faith.

persecution: The intentional harassment or abuse of a person or group by another person or group, often because of religious differences.

CLOSING PRAYER

"Lord God, thank you for every heart that has been on this journey. Thank you for everything we have learned about you and your love for us. Help us to see how your love and your plan change the world. Help us to live out our part of your story of salvation. Help us to see your constant action, your calling for us, and the destiny of heaven that lies ahead. In Jesus' name, we pray. Amen."

Glossary

ADVOCATE – From a Latin word meaning "to call to one's aid"; another name for the Holy Spirit.

ANOINT – From a Latin word meaning "to smear with oil." Anointing is a sacred ceremonial practice in which holy oil is smeared on someone as a sign that they are set apart for a special purpose.

APOSTLE – From a Greek word meaning "one who is sent." The original twelve Apostles were chosen by Jesus to preach the Gospel and make disciples of all nations.

ARK OF THE COVENANT – The wooden, gold-covered chest that held the two stone tablets of the Ten Commandments and other sacred objects of the Israelites.

ASCENSION, THE – From a Latin word meaning "to go up." The Ascension occurred forty days after the Resurrection when the Apostles witnessed Jesus go up into heaven.

BAPTISM – From a Greek word meaning "to immerse." Through Baptism, we become a new creation, an adopted son or daughter of God, and an official member of the Church. The graces of Baptism help us to live and share in God's love.

BIBLE – From the Greek word *biblia*, which means "collection of books." The Bible contains seventy-three books of many different types.

CATHOLIC – A word meaning "universal"; the name for the Church instituted by Jesus and passed down through the successors of the Apostles.

CHRISTIAN – A follower of Christ who has been baptized in his name.

CHURCH – The whole assembly of baptized Christians throughout the world who profess the same faith in Jesus Christ.

CONCUPISCENCE – The desire or inclination to commit sin.

COVENANT – From a Latin word meaning "to agree on." More than a contract, a covenant is an exchange of persons that helps establish an ongoing relationship.

CROSS – In the Roman Empire, crucifixion was a form of execution carried out by nailing or binding a person to a wooden cross. Jesus' Cross has become a universal Christian symbol of his sacrifice and victory over sin and death.

EXILE – To be forced from your native home and have to live somewhere else. During the Exile period, God's people were conquered by their enemies and led away from the Promised Land by their captors, and they lived in exile for many years.

FALL, THE – The event in Genesis when Adam and Eve disobeyed God and "fell" from grace.

GARDEN OF EDEN – Also called "Paradise." God made this special place for Adam and Eve to live in before the Fall.

GOSPEL – From the Old English words meaning "good news." In the New Testament, the four Gospels are the four books that detail the life, teachings, miracles, death, and Resurrection of Jesus.

GRACE – The divine assistance freely given to us by God, which we did not need to earn. Grace allows us to respond to God's call to become his children.

"I AM WHO I AM" – The holy name of God, first spoken to Moses. "I AM" or "I AM WHO I AM" is the English translation of the four-letter Hebrew word YHWH (commonly pronounced "Yahweh").

INCARNATION, THE – From the word "incarnate," which means to take on flesh or human form. Through the Incarnation, God the Son assumed a human body, was born of Mary, and became man.

INSPIRED – From a Latin word meaning "to breathe into." The Holy Spirit guided the human authors of the Bible as they wrote the truth God wants us to know for our salvation.

ISRAELITES – The descendants of the Patriarch Jacob (whose other name was Israel). Jacob's twelve sons were the ancestors of the twelve tribes of Israel.

JEWS – Another name for the Israelite people, or "men of Judah," used in the period of the Exile and after.

JUDGES – The twelve leaders of Israel who were chosen by God to help defend the Israelites from their enemies.

LAST SUPPER – The Passover meal that Jesus ate with his Apostles on the same night as his betrayal and arrest. It was during this meal that he instituted the Eucharist.

LEPERS – People who contracted the disease of leprosy. According to the Law of Moses, lepers were unclean and had to live away from other people.

MANNA – The heavenly food that God provided to sustain the Israelites while they wandered in the desert. Manna was white and sweet and could be made into cakes.

MARTYRDOM – From a Greek word meaning "witness." A martyr gives up his or her life in defense of the Faith.

MESSIAH – From the Hebrew word that means "anointed one." The Messiah was prophesied to be as the one who would deliver the Jewish people from oppression.

MORALITY – The principles that determine whether something is right or wrong, good or evil.

NEW AND EVERLASTING COVENANT – The final, perpetual covenant that God made with the entire human family through Jesus Christ, making it possible for us to dwell with him in heaven for eternity.

NEW TESTAMENT – The latter part of the Bible that details the life, death, and Resurrection of Jesus Christ, along with the early history of his Church.

OLD TESTAMENT – The first part of the Bible, which details Creation, the Fall, and God's ongoing attempts to repair his relationship with humanity.

ORIGINAL SIN – The "stain" of sin that we inherited from Adam and Eve, which means we are born in a "state of sin" and require redemption.

OUR FATHER – Also called the "Lord's Prayer." This prayer that Jesus taught his disciples is considered a summary of the whole Gospel.

PASSION, THE – The time of Jesus' suffering, from his agony in the Garden of Gethsemane through his arrest, trial, and crucifixion.

PASSOVER – The Jewish feast that commemorates the night when God "passed over" the Israelite homes in Egypt, protecting their children from death and freeing them from slavery.

PATRIARCH – The male head of a family or tribe, often the eldest or most respected man in the family. A matriarch is the female head of a family or tribe. The Patriarchs of the Israelites are Abraham, Isaac, and Jacob.

PERSECUTION – The intentional harassment or abuse of a person or group by another person or group, often because of religious differences.

PLAGUES – A series of devastating catastrophes that fell upon the Egyptians after Pharaoh refused to let the Israelites go and worship God.

PROMISED LAND – The region that God promised to give to Abraham and his descendants as an inheritance. Other terms for this area are "Israel," "the Levant," "Palestine," and "Canaan."

PROPHETS – Individuals chosen by God to proclaim God's will to the people and call everyone to live according to the covenant. In biblical times, they often played an important role as inspired advisors to kings.

REDEEMER, REDEMPTION – From a Latin word meaning "to buy back." Jesus is our Redeemer because he paid the price for us with his own blood and saved us from sin and death.

REVELATION – Divine truth that God communicates to us through his Word (Scripture) and the teachings handed down to us (Tradition).

SACRED SCRIPTURE – The collection of ancient biblical texts that are inspired by God and reveal his nature and presence to his people.

SALVATION – Our deliverance through Jesus Christ from the powers of sin and death.

SALVATION HISTORY – The events that reveal God's redemptive plan in human history, culminating in Jesus Christ, who completely reveals the Father to us.

SAVIOR – Jesus Christ, the one who delivers us from the consequences of sin and death.

TABERNACLE – The portable tent that the Israelites used for worship in the desert. It housed the Ark of the Covenant.

TEN COMMANDMENTS – Ten laws that God gave the Israelites to teach them how to live and worship as a free people.

TRINITY – The three distinct Persons who make up the single divine nature of God: the Father, the Son, and the Holy Spirit.

TRANSFIGURED – Transformed into something better or more beautiful.

WORSHIP – To honor and show reverence to God alone.

FURTHER RESOURCES

Catholic Prayers 129

The Rosary. 132

The Divine Mercy Chaplet 134

Lectio Divina. 135

The Ten Commandments 136

The Beatitudes. 137

An Examination of Conscience for Middle School. 138

Verses to Help on Hard Days. 141

Catholic Prayers

You may already know some of these prayers. Practice one or two every day. When you've memorized them, you'll be able to pray them anytime—at Mass, when you say the Rosary, when you or a friend needs help, or whenever you want to say thank you to God.

THE OUR FATHER

Our Father, who art in heaven, hallowed be thy name; thy kingdom come, thy will be done, on earth as it is in heaven. Give us this day our daily bread, and forgive us our trespasses as we forgive those who trespass against us; and lead us not into temptation, but deliver us from evil. Amen.

THE HAIL MARY

Hail Mary, full of grace, the Lord is with thee. Blessed art thou among women, and blessed is the fruit of thy womb, Jesus. Holy Mary, Mother of God, pray for us sinners, now and at the hour of our death. Amen.

THE GLORY BE

Glory be to the Father, and to the Son, and to the Holy Spirit, as it was in the beginning, is now, and ever shall be, world without end. Amen.

THE APOSTLES' CREED

I believe in God, the Father almighty, Creator of heaven and earth, and in Jesus Christ, his only Son, our Lord, who was conceived by the Holy Spirit, born of the Virgin Mary, suffered under Pontius Pilate, was crucified, died, and was buried; he descended into hell; on the third day he rose again from the dead; he ascended into heaven, and is seated at the right hand of God the Father almighty; from there he will come to judge the living and the dead. I believe in the Holy Spirit, the holy catholic Church, the communion of saints, the forgiveness of sins, the resurrection of the body, and life everlasting. Amen.

FATIMA PRAYER

O my Jesus, forgive us our sins, save us from the fires of hell, and lead all souls to heaven, especially those in most need of thy mercy.

ROSARY PRAYER

God, whose only begotten Son, by his life, death, and Resurrection, has purchased for us the rewards of eternal life, grant, we beseech thee, that meditating upon these mysteries of the Most Holy Rosary of the Blessed Virgin Mary, we may imitate what they contain and obtain what they promise, through the same Christ our Lord. Amen.

HAIL, HOLY QUEEN

Hail, Holy Queen, Mother of mercy, our life, our sweetness, and our hope. To thee do we cry, poor banished children of Eve; to thee do we send up our sighs, mourning and weeping in this valley of tears. Turn, then, most gracious advocate, thine eyes of mercy toward us, and after this, our exile, show unto us the blessed fruit of thy womb, Jesus. O clement, O loving, O sweet Virgin Mary.

V. Pray for us, O Holy Mother of God.
R. That we may be made worthy of the promises of Christ.
Amen.

THE *MEMORARE*

Remember, O most gracious Virgin Mary, that never was it known that anyone who fled to thy protection, implored thy help, or sought thine intercession was left unaided. Inspired with this confidence, I fly unto thee, O Virgin of virgins, my Mother; to thee do I come, before thee I stand, sinful and sorrowful. O Mother of the Word Incarnate, despise not my petitions, but in thy mercy, hear and answer me. Amen.

THE *ANGELUS*

V. The angel of the Lord declared unto Mary,
R. And she conceived by the Holy Spirit.
Hail Mary …

V. Behold the handmaid of the Lord.
R. Be it done unto me according to thy Word.
Hail Mary …

V. And the Word was made flesh,
R. And dwelt among us.
Hail Mary …

V. Pray for us, O Holy Mother of God,
R. That we may be made worthy of the promises of Christ.

Let us pray: Pour forth, we beseech thee, O Lord, thy grace into our hearts, that we, to whom the Incarnation of Christ, thy Son, was made known by the message of an angel, may by his passion and cross be brought to the glory of his Resurrection, through the same Christ our Lord. Amen.

PRAYER TO ST. MICHAEL
St. Michael the Archangel, defend us in battle. Be our protection against the wickedness and snares of the devil. May God rebuke him, we humbly pray, and do thou, O Prince of the Heavenly Host, by the power of God, cast into hell Satan and all the evil spirits, who prowl throughout the world seeking the ruin of souls. Amen.

PRAYER TO YOUR GUARDIAN ANGEL
Angel of God, my guardian dear, to whom God's love commits me here, ever this day (night) be at my side, to light and guard, to rule and guide. Amen.

MORNING OFFERING
O Jesus, through the Immaculate Heart of Mary,
I offer you my prayers, works, joys, and sufferings of this day
for all the intentions of your Sacred Heart
in union with the Holy Sacrifice of the Mass throughout the world,
for the salvation of souls, the reparation of sins, the reunion of all Christians,
and in particular for the intentions of the Holy Father this month.
Amen.

The Rosary

The Rosary gives us a chance to spend time with Our Lady and think about the events of Jesus' life, death, and Resurrection. For each mystery, put yourself into the scene, asking Mary to help you see it through her eyes. The Rosary is a beautiful way to pray with Mary—whether you pray by yourself, with your family, or with friends.

Rosary beads are special. They are often blessed by a priest or deacon, and so we should always treat the beads with respect and affection. (That's why, while the beads may look like a necklace, we don't wear them.) We hold the beads in our hands and keep count of the Rosary prayers with our fingers.

Our Lady gave the first Rosary to St. Dominic in 1208! For the text of the individual prayers, see pages 129–130.

THE MYSTERIES OF THE ROSARY

The Joyful Mysteries
1. The Annunciation
2. The Visitation
3. The Nativity
4. The Presentation
5. The Finding of Jesus in the Temple

The Luminous Mysteries
1. The Baptism of Christ in the Jordan
2. The Manifestation of Christ at the Wedding of Cana
3. The Proclamation of the Kingdom of God, with His Call to Conversion
4. The Transfiguration
5. The Institution of the Eucharist

The Sorrowful Mysteries
1. The Agony in the Garden
2. The Scourging at the Pillar
3. The Crowning with Thorns
4. The Carrying of the Cross
5. The Crucifixion

The Glorious Mysteries
1. The Resurrection
2. The Ascension
3. The Descent of the Holy Spirit
4. The Assumption
5. The Coronation of the Blessed Virgin Mary

HOW TO PRAY THE ROSARY

For the text of the individual prayers listed here, see "Catholic Prayers" above.

1. Holding the rosary beads, make the Sign of the Cross.

2. Pray the Apostles' Creed (on the crucifix).

3. Pray an Our Father (first bead).

4. Pray three Hail Marys (second through fourth beads).

5. Pray the Glory Be and the (optional) Fatima Prayer (fifth bead).

6. Announce the first mystery, and then pray the Our Father.

7. Pray ten Hail Marys on the next decade (ten beads), meditating on the mystery.

8. On the next single bead, pray the Glory Be and the (optional) Fatima Prayer.

9. On the same bead, announce the next mystery and pray the Our Father.

10. Repeat steps 7 to 9 for each of the four remaining mysteries.

11. After the fifth mystery, pray the Hail, Holy Queen (on the rosary centerpiece).

12. Conclude with the Rosary Prayer, and make the Sign of the Cross.

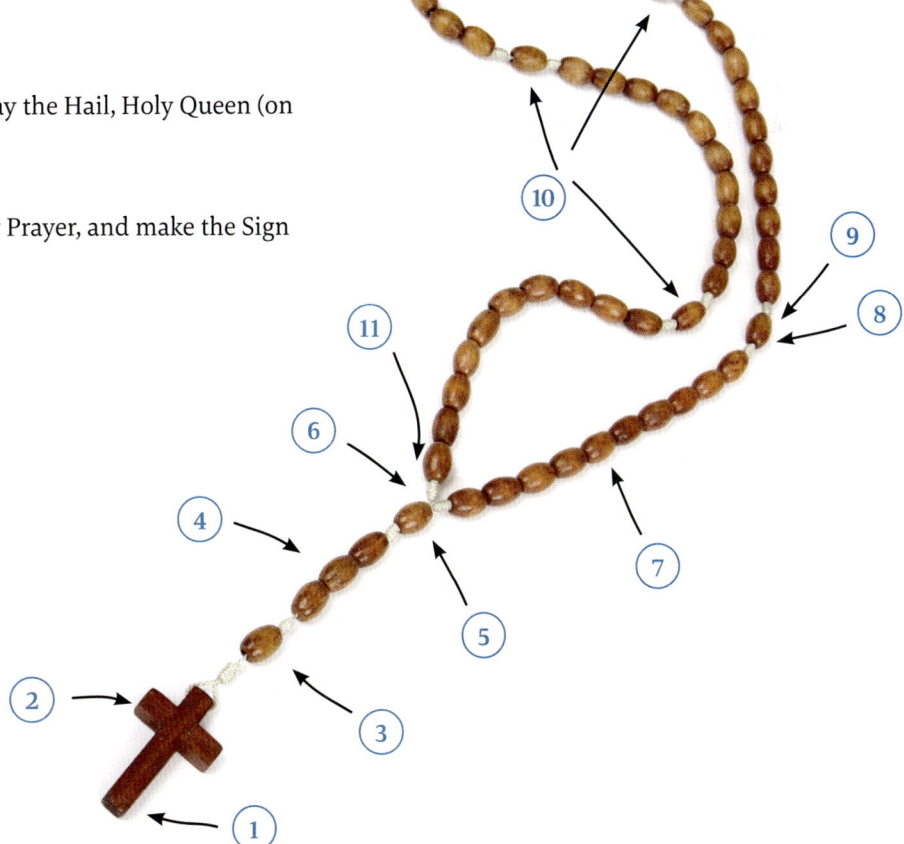

Further Resources | 133

The Divine Mercy Chaplet

The Divine Mercy Chaplet gives us a chance to meditate on Jesus' Passion and infinite Divine Mercy. We use rosary beads to keep count as we pray.

Our Lord gave the chaplet prayers to St. Faustina in September 1935. For the text of the individual prayers, see pages 129–130.

1. Using rosary beads, begin with the Sign of the Cross, one Our Father, one Hail Mary, and the Apostles' Creed.

2. On each Our Father bead, pray, "Eternal Father, I offer you the Body and Blood, Soul and Divinity of your dearly beloved Son, our Lord Jesus Christ, in atonement for our sins and those of the whole world."

3. On each Hail Mary bead, pray, "For the sake of his sorrowful passion, have mercy on us and on the whole world."

4. Repeat these prayers on each decade. End by praying three times, "Holy God, Holy Mighty One, Holy Immortal One, have mercy on us and on the whole world."

Lectio Divina
(LEK-tsee-oh dee-VEE-nah)

Lectio divina (which means "divine reading" in Latin) is the traditional Catholic practice of reading and praying with Scripture. You can begin with a favorite Bible story, the "Remember This!" verse in your *Encounter* lesson, or one of the readings from "Find Out More."

With *lectio divina*, just like with the Rosary, it helps to imagine that you are in the scene. For example, you could be helping your family collect manna in the desert (Exodus 16:14–21), listening to Jesus preach the Sermon on the Mount (Luke 6:17–49), or escaping a shipwreck with St. Paul (Acts 27).

As you pray, follow these four steps:

Step 1: *Lectio* (reading)
Begin with the Sign of the Cross and ask the Holy Spirit to assist you in this time of prayer. Next, read a selected passage from Scripture slowly and intentionally. If possible, read the passage aloud. Listen to the words as if God is speaking to you directly, immersing yourself in the passage. If needed, you can read the passage a second time.

Step 2: *Meditatio* (meditation)
The second step is to meditate on the passage you just read. It is helpful to focus on particular words or verses that spoke to you or caught your attention during the reading. Like the Virgin Mary (see Luke 2:19), ponder the Word of God in your heart, seeking to encounter him and discern what he might be saying to you.

Step 3: *Oratio* (prayer)
In prayer, we not only speak to God but also listen to what he is saying. You can use a formal prayer from the tradition of the Church, saying the words slowly and paying attention to what the prayer is telling you about God and about your relationship with him. You may also pray in your own words, asking God for greater understanding of the Scripture passage that you just read. Ask if he wants you to make changes in your life or in your faith journey.

Step 4: *Contemplatio* (contemplation)
Contemplation is resting in God's presence and allowing him to arrange your thoughts and prayer. Let God enter and change your heart and mind according to his will. Like anything new, *lectio divina* may take a little practice. However, if you practice it faithfully and give God a few minutes of your time, you will start to see a real difference in your spiritual life.

The Ten Commandments

1. I am the Lord your God: you shall not have strange gods before me.

2. You shall not take the name of the Lord your God in vain.

3. Remember to keep holy the Lord's Day.

4. Honor your father and your mother.

5. You shall not kill.

6. You shall not commit adultery.

7. You shall not steal.

8. You shall not bear false witness against your neighbor.

9. You shall not covet your neighbor's wife.

10. You shall not covet your neighbor's goods.

In their extraordinary encounters on Mount Sinai, God gave Moses the Ten Commandments (*Catechism,* following CCC 2051) and all the Law, speaking to Moses from heaven and writing the commandments on stone tablets with his own finger (Exodus 31:18). The commandments are the ground rules for human life. In them, God is telling us how to worship him and live with other people.

It is important to understand that following these commandments is the minimum expected of a Christian. Jesus reminds us of the importance of the Ten Commandments when he speaks to the rich young man (Matthew 19:16–22), and he adds that the young man must surrender everything and follow him if he wants to gain eternal life. If we want the same, we too must go beyond the bare minimum and live each day putting Jesus and our faith first.

Some Christian denominations number the Ten Commandments differently than we do as Catholics. Our Tradition uses the division listed above, given to us by St. Augustine. This list is the one established by the early Church and has been handed on to us through the centuries.

If you can commit the commandments to memory and live them out daily, you're well on your way to sainthood!

The Beatitudes

> Blessed are the poor in spirit, for theirs is the kingdom of heaven.
>
> Blessed are those who mourn, for they shall be comforted.
>
> Blessed are the meek, for they shall inherit the earth.
>
> Blessed are those who hunger and thirst for righteousness, for they shall be satisfied.
>
> Blessed are the merciful, for they shall receive mercy.
>
> Blessed are the pure in heart, for they shall see God.
>
> Blessed are the peacemakers, for they shall be called sons of God.
>
> Blessed are those who are persecuted for righteousness' sake, for theirs is the kingdom of heaven.
>
> Blessed are you when men revile you and persecute you and utter all kinds of evil against you falsely on my account. Rejoice and be glad, for your reward is great in heaven.

The word *beatitude* means "blessed." The Beatitudes are not laws or rules like the Ten Commandments; rather, they show us what God's love looks like in practice—what the Catechism calls "an order of happiness and grace, of beauty and peace" (CCC 2546).

It might already make sense to us that someone who is merciful or a peacemaker may be considered blessed. But why would we ever think of a person in mourning or a person suffering persecution as "blessed"? The answer is found in Jesus. The Beatitudes are Jesus' self-portrait. During his time on earth, Jesus embodied the Beatitudes perfectly: he was poor, humble, righteous, merciful, pure—and the Prince of Peace. He mourned the sorrows of our sinful world, and he suffered persecution for preaching the Kingdom of God. He was ultimately put to death—but through the Resurrection, Jesus reveals the reality of eternal life with the Father. As St. Paul says, "I consider that the sufferings of this present time are not worth comparing with the glory that is to be revealed to us" (Romans 8:18). The Beatitudes teach us that, though we all experience struggles and sufferings in our Christian life on earth, those who follow Jesus' example and live as faithful disciples will receive eternal glory in heaven.

If we want to live more like Jesus in our ordinary circumstances, we can look to the Beatitudes as a starting point. You can find the Beatitudes in Matthew 5:3–12; they are the opening words to Jesus' Sermon on the Mount.

An Examination of Conscience for Middle School

An examination of conscience is a tool we use to be aware of how we have sinned since our last Confession so that we can repent and know what we need to confess. We can also use it daily before bedtime as a way to check in on our souls.

A sin is an offense against God that wounds our relationship with him and others. When we do an examination of conscience, we quiet ourselves, ask the Holy Spirit to show us how and when we fell into sin, and take time to remember our thoughts, words, and deeds. We don't do this to feel bad about ourselves or to be discouraged. We do it so we can be truly sorry for our sins and know how we want to act in the future, so we can receive the forgiveness and healing that God wants to give us.

As we examine our consciences, we also ask for the grace to avoid sin and the near occasion of sin (the situations that make it easy to fall into sin) in the future.

Remember that we must confess all mortal sins in Confession. These are sins that reject God's grace, his life in our souls. Mortal sins can mean the difference between heaven and hell. A sin is mortal if:

- We knew it was serious.
- We knew it was wrong.
- We freely chose to do it anyway.

The Ten Commandments are a clear and direct way for us to examine our consciences because when we break these commandments, we fall into sin. Here is an examination of conscience from the Ten Commandments that can help you experience God's mercy and healing in your life.*

---

* This examination of conscience from the Ten Commandments has been reprinted by permission from *Renewed by Jesus: My Guide to Reconciliation*, by Colin and Aimee MacIver (West Chester, PA: Ascension, 2023), 52–59. Two other examinations of conscience—from the Beatitudes and from the seven deadly sins—can also be found there.

First Commandment: "I am the Lord your God. You shall not have strange gods before me."
- Did I try to make God the most important thing in my life?
- Did I act like other things, activities, or people are more important than God?
- Did I spend time with God each day in prayer?
- Did I thank God for the good things he has given me?
- Did I receive Holy Communion with mortal sins that I have not confessed yet?

Second Commandment: "You shall not take the name of the Lord your God in vain."
- Did I always use God's name with love and respect?
- Did I use God's name out of anger or as a curse?
- Did I speak badly about God, the saints, or any other holy person or thing?
- Did I use bad language or curse words?

Third Commandment: "Remember to keep holy the Lord's Day."
- Did I miss Mass on a Sunday or Holy Day of Obligation on purpose without a good reason (like being sick or not having a ride)?
- Did I complain about going to Mass?
- Did I pay attention at Mass as best I could? Did I say the responses, pray, and sing?
- Did I fast (no food or drink except water) for one hour before receiving Holy Communion?
- Did I rest on Sundays?

Fourth Commandment: "Honor your father and your mother."
- Did I show love and respect to my parents or the adults who take care of me?
- Did I disobey them? Did I get angry or talk back to them?
- Did I try to be thankful for what my parents do for me?
- Did I help my family at home? Did I complain about chores?
- Did I argue or fight with my brothers or sisters? Am I kind to them?
- Did I respect and obey other adults in charge (priests, nuns, teachers, police, etc.)?
- Did I obey the rules at school?
- Did I do my best on homework and other schoolwork?

Fifth Commandment: "You shall not kill."
- Did I hurt anyone on purpose?
- Did I make fun of others or call them names?
- Did I lose my temper or get angry at anyone?

- Did I not forgive someone?
- Did I leave out anyone on purpose?
- Did I talk badly about others or gossip?
- Did I share what I can with others, especially those who have less than I do?
- Did I try to take care of my body?

Sixth and Ninth Commandments: "You shall not commit adultery." "You shall not covet your neighbor's wife."
- Did I try to treat my body and others' bodies with respect?
- Did I think about disrespectful things on purpose?
- Did I listen to or tell disrespectful jokes?
- Did I look at disrespectful images, videos, TV shows, or movies?

Seventh and Tenth Commandments: "You shall not steal." "You shall not covet your neighbor's goods."
- Did I steal anything?
- Did I take something without permission? Did I purposely not return something?
- Did I damage someone else's things?
- Was I greedy or selfish?
- Did I share what I can, especially with those who have less than I do?
- Am I thankful for what I have?
- Am I jealous of what others have or what they can do?

Eighth Commandment: "You shall not bear false witness against your neighbor."
- Did I lie? Did I tell half the truth?
- Did I blame others for something that I did?
- Did I spread rumors about someone?
- Did I tell secrets?
- Did I cheat on school work or in a game?
- Did I keep my promises?
- Did I keep silent when I should have said something?

Verses to Help on Hard Days

Living the Catholic life isn't easy. Being a Christian in today's world requires a lot of patience, especially with challenges at school, on social media—even in your own family. It also requires confidence in God's loving care for you. Below are some passages from the Bible that speak to some of the feelings and struggles you may face. They are good passages to reflect on in prayer, and they can offer you hope and deepen your confidence in God's loving care for you.

Happy reading!

WHY BOTHER BEING HOLY?

"You are a chosen race, a royal priesthood, a holy nation, God's own people, that you may declare the wonderful deeds of him who called you out of darkness into his marvelous light." —1 Peter 2:9

"As he who called you is holy, be holy yourselves in all your conduct; since it is written, 'You shall be holy, for I am holy.'" —1 Peter 1:15–16

"Strive for peace with all men, and for the holiness without which no one will see the Lord." —Hebrews 12:14

NEED SOME CONFIDENCE BEFORE YOU START YOUR DAY?

"I can do all things in him who strengthens me." —Philippians 4:13

"The Lord is my light and my salvation;
  whom shall I fear?
The Lord is the stronghold of my life;
  of whom shall I be afraid?" —Psalm 27:1–3

"The Lord will be your confidence and will keep your foot from being caught." —Proverbs 3:26

CAN'T FIND THE RIGHT WORDS WHEN YOU PRAY?

"[Jesus said,] 'Pray then like this:

Our Father who art in heaven,
Hallowed be thy name.
Thy kingdom come.
Thy will be done
  on earth as it is in heaven.
Give us this day our daily bread;
and forgive us our trespasses

as we forgive those who trespass against us;
and lead us not into temptation,
But deliver us from evil.'" —Matthew 6:9–13

"The Spirit helps us in our weakness; for we do not know how to pray as we ought, but the Spirit himself intercedes for us with sighs too deep for words." —Romans 8:26

"The LORD is near to all who call upon him, to all who call on him in truth." —Psalm 145:18

AFRAID THAT GOD WILL ABANDON YOU OR STOP LOVING YOU?

"God so loved the world that he gave his only-begotten Son, that whoever believes in him should not perish but have eternal life." —John 3:16

"The steadfast love of the LORD never ceases;
   his mercies never come to an end;
they are new every morning;
   great is your faithfulness." —Lamentations 3:22–23

"For I am sure that neither death, nor life, nor angels, nor principalities, nor things present, nor things to come, nor powers, nor height, nor depth, nor anything else in all creation, will be able to separate us from the love of God in Christ Jesus our Lord." —Romans 8:38–39

WONDERING WHETHER GOD IS REALLY LISTENING TO YOUR PRAYERS?

"[Jesus said,] 'Ask, and it will be given you; seek, and you will find; knock, and it will be opened to you. For every one who asks receives, and he who seeks finds, and to him who knocks it will be opened.'" —Matthew 7:7–8

"You will call upon me and come and pray to me, and I will hear you. You will seek me and find me; when you seek me with all your heart, I will be found by you, says the Lord." —Jeremiah 29:12–13

"This is the confidence which we have in him, that if we ask anything according to his will he hears us." —1 John 5:14

WORRIED ABOUT WHAT THE FUTURE HOLDS OR AFRAID OF TRUSTING GOD WITH YOUR WHOLE LIFE?

"I know the plans I have for you, says the Lord, plans for welfare and not for evil, to give you a future and a hope." —Jeremiah 29:11

"I am sure that he who began a good work in you will bring it to completion at the day of Jesus Christ." —Philippians 1:6

"We know that in everything God works for good with those who love him, who are called according to his purpose." —Romans 8:28

WANT TO KNOW THE SECRET TO BEING GREAT IN GOD'S EYES?

"The Lord sees not as man sees; man looks on the outward appearance, but the Lord looks on the heart." —1 Samuel 16:7

"[Jesus] sat down and called the Twelve and he said to them, 'If any one would be first, he must be last of all and servant of all.' And he took a child, and put him in the midst of them; and taking him in his arms, he said to them, 'Whoever receives one such child in my name receives me; and whoever receives me, receives not me but him who sent me.'" —Mark 9:35–37

"[Jesus said,] 'Let the greatest among you become as the youngest, and the leader as one who serves.'" —Luke 22:26

FEELING DOWN ON YOURSELF BECAUSE YOU KEEP MESSING UP?

"Since all have sinned and fall short of the glory of God, they are justified by his grace as a gift, through the redemption which is in Christ Jesus." —Romans 3:23–24

"[The Lord] said to me, 'My grace is sufficient for you, for my power is made perfect in weakness.'" —2 Corinthians 12:9

"If any one is in Christ, he is a new creation; the old has passed away, behold, the new has come." —2 Corinthians 5:17

AFRAID TO CONFESS YOUR SINS?

"If we confess our sins, he is faithful and just, and will forgive our sins and cleanse us from all unrighteousness." —1 John 1:9

"I acknowledged my sin to you,
    and I did not hide my iniquity;
I said, 'I will confess my transgressions to the Lord';
    then you forgave the guilt of my sin." —Psalm 32:5

"He who conceals his transgressions will not prosper,
    but he who confesses and forsakes them will obtain mercy." —Proverbs 28:13

NERVOUS ABOUT A PRESENTATION OR SOCIAL SITUATION?

"Fear not, for I am with you, be not dismayed, for I am your God; I will strengthen you, I will help you, I will uphold you." —Isaiah 41:10

"Cast all your anxieties on him, for he cares about you." —1 Peter 5:7

"Have no anxiety about anything, but in everything by prayer and supplication with thanksgiving let your requests be made known to God. And the peace of God, which passes all understanding, will keep your hearts and your minds in Christ Jesus." —Philippians 4:6–7

UPSET ABOUT THINGS THAT PEOPLE ARE SAYING AT HOME, AT SCHOOL, OR ON SOCIAL MEDIA?

"Let all bitterness and wrath and anger and clamor and slander be put away from you, with all malice, and be kind to one another, tenderhearted, forgiving one another, as God in Christ forgave you." —Ephesians 4:31–32

"[Jesus said,] 'Judge not, and you will not be judged; condemn not, and you will not be condemned; forgive, and you will be forgiven; give, and it will be given to you. ... For the measure you give will be the measure you get back.'" —Luke 6:37–38

"[Jesus said,] 'Whatever you wish that men would do to you, do so to them.'" —Matthew 7:12

NOT SURE WHAT TO DO ABOUT YOUR "ENEMIES" OR HOW TO DEAL WITH PEOPLE WHO HURT YOU OR MAKE YOU ANGRY?

"[Jesus said,] 'I say to you that hear, Love your enemies, do good to those who hate you, bless those who curse you, pray for those who abuse you. ... And as you wish that men would do to you, do so to them.'" —Luke 6:27–28, 31

"'If your enemy is hungry, feed him; if he is thirsty, give him drink; for by so doing you will heap burning coals upon his head.' Do not be overcome by evil, but overcome evil with good." —Romans 12:20

"Be angry but do not sin; do not let the sun go down on your anger." —Ephesians 4:26

"Let no evil talk come out of your mouths, but only such as is good for edifying, as fits the occasion, that it may impart grace to those who hear." —Ephesians 4:29

READY TO GIVE UP HOPE THAT CERTAIN FRIENDS OR FAMILY WILL EVER FOLLOW GOD?

"[The disciples asked,] 'Who then can be saved?' But Jesus looked at them and said to them, 'With men this is impossible, but with God all things are possible.'" —Matthew 19:25–26

"God our Savior ... desires all men to be saved and to come to the knowledge of the truth." —1 Timothy 2:3–4

"The Lord is not slow about his promise as some count slowness, but is forbearing toward you, not wishing that any should perish, but that all should reach repentance." —2 Peter 3:9

FEELING LIKE NO ONE WILL LISTEN TO YOU BECAUSE YOU'RE TOO YOUNG?

"Let no one despise your youth, but set the believers an example in speech and conduct, in love, in faith, in purity." —1 Timothy 4:12

"The Lord said to me, 'Do not say, "I am only a youth"; for to all to whom I send you you shall go, and whatever I command you you shall speak. Be not afraid of them, for I am with you to deliver you.'" —Jeremiah 1:7

FEELING HOPELESS?

"The Lord is near to the brokenhearted, and saves the crushed in spirit." —Psalm 34:18

"Be strong and of good courage, do not fear or be in dread … for it is the Lord your God who goes with you; he will not fail you or forsake you." —Deuteronomy 31:6

"May the God of hope fill you with all joy and peace in believing, so that by the power of the Holy Spirit you may abound in hope." —Romans 15:13

FEELING TIRED OR WEAK?

"[Jesus said,] 'Come to me, all who labor and are heavy laden, and I will give you rest. Take my yoke upon you, and learn from me; for I am gentle and lowly in heart, and you will find rest for your souls. For my yoke is easy, and my burden is light.'" —Matthew 11: 28–30

"The Lord … gives power to the faint,
   and to him who has no might he increases strength. …
They who wait for the Lord shall renew their strength,
   they shall mount up with wings like eagles,
they shall run and not be weary,
   they shall walk and not faint." —Isaiah 40:28–29, 31

"I can do all things in him who strengthens me." —Philippians 4:13

FEELING ALONE OR DOWN?

"Be strong and of good courage; be not frightened, neither be dismayed; for the Lord your God is with you wherever you go." —Joshua 1:9

"Where shall I go from your Spirit?
   Or where shall I flee from your presence?
If I ascend to heaven, you are there!
   If I make my bed in Sheol [the abode of the dead], you are there!
If I take the wings of the morning
   and dwell in the uttermost parts of the sea,
even there your hand shall lead me,

> and your right hand shall hold me.
> If I say, 'Let only darkness cover me,
> > and the light about me be night,'
> even the darkness is not dark to you,
> > the night is bright as the day;
> > for darkness is as light with you." —Psalm 139:7–12

"Blessed be the God and Father of our Lord Jesus Christ, the Father of mercies and God of all comfort, who comforts us in all our affliction, so that we may be able to comfort those who are in any affliction, with the comfort with which we ourselves are comforted by God." —2 Corinthians 1:3–4

FEELING TIRED OF DOING THE RIGHT THING?

"And let us not grow weary in well-doing, for in due season we shall reap, if we do not lose heart." —Galatians 6:9

> "Do not fret because of the wicked,
> > be not envious of wrongdoers!
> For they will soon fade like the grass,
> > and wither like the green herb.
> Trust in the Lord, and do good;
> > so you will dwell in the land, and be nourished in safety.
> Take delight in the Lord,
> > and he will give you the desires of your heart.
> Commit your way to the Lord;
> > trust in him, and he will act." —Psalm 37:1–5

"My beloved brethren, be steadfast, immovable, always abounding in the work of the Lord, knowing that in the Lord your labor is not in vain." —1 Corinthians 15:58

FEELING OVERWHELMED BY TEMPTATION?

"No temptation has overtaken you that is not common to man. God is faithful, and he will not let you be tempted beyond your strength, but with the temptation will also provide the way of escape, that you may be able to endure it." —1 Corinthians 10:13

"[Jesus said,] 'Watch and pray that you may not enter into temptation; the spirit indeed is willing, but the flesh is weak.'" —Matthew 26:41

"God did not give us a spirit of timidity but a spirit of power and love and self-control." —2 Timothy 1:7

IS REMAINING PURE A STRUGGLE FOR YOU OR YOUR FRIENDS?

"Whatever is true, whatever is honorable, whatever is just, whatever is pure, whatever is lovely, whatever is gracious, if there is any excellence, if there is anything worthy of praise, think about these things." —Philippians 4:8

"This is the will of God, your sanctification: that you abstain from immorality; that each one of you know how to control his own body in holiness and honor, not in the passion of lust like heathens who do not know God. … For God has not called us for uncleanness, but in holiness."
—1 Thessalonians 4:3–5, 7

"Be content with what you have; for he has said, 'I will never fail you or forsake you.' Hence we can confidently say, 'The Lord is my helper, I will not be afraid; what can man do to me?'"
—Hebrews 13:5–6

About the Authors and Presenters

MEET THE AUTHORS

MARK HART, affectionately known as the Bible Geek, is a best-selling author, award-winning producer, Catholic radio personality, and highly sought-after speaker. He proudly serves as the CIO (Chief Innovation Officer) of Life Teen International. Mark and his wife, Melanie, have four children and live in Phoenix, Arizona.

COLIN and **AIMEE MACIVER** teach theology at St. Scholastica Academy in Covington, Louisiana, where they serve as the campus minister and service director, respectively. Their decades of combined experience in ministry include youth ministry, Confirmation prep, speaking, training, visual art, and music ministry. Colin and Aimee have authored a number of popular programs with Ascension over the years, with *Receiving Jesus: My Guide to the Mass* and *Envision: Theology of the Body for Middle School* being two of their latest projects.

MEET THE PRESENTERS

CHIKA ANYANWU is a Catholic evangelist, former Confirmation coordinator/youth and young adult minister, and the author of *My Encounter: How I Met Jesus in Prayer.* Whether speaking nationally or internationally about prayer, human dignity, or being a 30-something single woman, she always puts the love and mercy of Jesus at the forefront of her message. Chika is a member of a beautiful Nigerian family, loves her coffee black, and desires sainthood for herself and you.

FR. FRANKIE CICERO is a priest of the Diocese of Phoenix, where he is the parochial vicar at St. Timothy's Catholic Church in Mesa, Arizona. He attended St. John Vianney Seminary in Denver, Colorado, and was ordained eight years later on June 16, 2018.

ASHLEY HINOJOSA is a doctoral student in moral theology at the University of Notre Dame. She received her BA in theology with a minor in pastoral ministry at the University of Dallas, an MA in theology through ND's McGrath Institute for Church Life's Echo Program (where she served in the Archdiocese of Galveston-Houston), and an MTS at Duke Divinity School. As a Catholic speaker and writer, Ashley has worked alongside organizations such as Life Teen, The Catholic Woman, and Ascension.

TANNER KALINA is cofounder of the *Saints Alive* podcast, an alumnus of FOCUS (Fellowship of Catholic University Students), and a team member of the National Eucharistic Congress. He hosts Ascension's *Envision: Theology of the Body for Middle School* series and has appeared in videos on Ascension Presents. He has also contributed video projects to FOCUS, EWTN, CatholicMatch, and YDisciple.

Encounter: The Bible Timeline for Middle School
Program Credits

EXECUTIVE PRODUCER & PUBLISHER
Jonathan Strate

GENERAL MANAGERS
Jeffrey Cole
Dcn. John Harden

PROJECT MANAGER
Veronica Salazar

PRODUCT MANAGER
Lauren McCann

SENIOR VIDEO PRODUCER
Matthew Pirrall

VIDEO CREATIVE DIRECTOR
Matthew Longua

Encounter Video Series

PRODUCTION COMPANY
Coronation Media

FEATURING
Mark Hart
Chika Anyanwu
Fr. Frankie Cicero
Ashley Hinojosa
Tanner Kalina

THEOLOGICAL CONSULTANTS
Jeffrey Cole
Dcn. John Harden
Carlos Taja

Encounter Written Materials

AUTHOR & WRITER
Mark Hart

CO-WRITERS
Aimee and Colin MacIver

CONTENT REVIEWERS
Jeffrey Cole
Dcn. John Harden
Lauren McCann
Carlos Taja
Lauren Welsh

GRAPHIC DESIGN
Sarah Stueve
Stella Ziegler

FEATURED ARTIST
Chris Lewis, BARITUS Catholic

PRINT EDITORIAL
Christina Eberle
Rebecca Robinson

MARKETING
Mark Leopold
Julia Morgensai